ARCHAEOLOGY BY EXPERIMENT

ARCHAEOLOGY BY EXPERIMENT

John Coles

Lecturer in *Archaeology*
University of *Cambridge*

CHARLES SCRIBNER'S SONS
NEW YORK

CONTENTS

PLATES

ACKNOWLEDGEMENTS

I have received advice and encouragement from a number of archaeologists and others, and I am grateful for this interest. Among many, I particularly thank Mr Hans-Ole Hansen, Historisk-Arkaeologisk Forsogscenter, Denmark, who has always been cooperative and helpful in sharing information. I thank Mrs Joan Green, Haddon Library, Cambridge, for much assistance in tracking down numerous rather obscure references, Mr Len Morley for photographic work, Mrs Edna Pilmer for typing, Miss Ann Douglas, Hutchinson, for helpful advice, and my wife Mona for help in compiling the index. Most of the illustrations have been redrawn from sources given in the captions to the drawings. Photographs and permissions have been kindly provided by Miss Felicity Kinross, BBC (Pl. 1); Dr M. L. Ryder (Pls. 2 and 4); Professor J. Malina, Brno (Pl. 3); the editors of *Skalk* (Pl. 5); the British Association for the Advancement of Science: Experimental Earthworks Committee (Pls. 6 and 7, and Fig. 13); Mr Brian Hobley (Pl. 8 and Fig. 15); Mr Thor Heyerdahl (Pls. 9 and 10); Professor Stuart Piggott (Pl. 13); Mr R. Savage, College of Art and Design, Cheltenham (Pl. 14); Mr Len Morley (Pl. 15); Time Inc. (Pl. 16); Mr G. F. Bryant, WEA, Barton-on-Humber, Lincolnshire (Pl. 17). Mr. P. J. Reynolds, Butser Ancient Farm Project, and Dr H. McKerrell, Edinburgh, have kindly read parts of the text.

JOHN COLES

TABLE OF EQUIVALENTS

1 micron = 0·001 millimetre
1 millimetre = 0·039 inch
1 centimetre = 0·394 inch
1 metre = 1·09 yard
1 kilometre = 0·62 mile
1 stadium = 185 metres
1 knot = 1 nautical mile = 1·85 kilometre
1 hectare = 2·47 acres
1 cubic metre = 35·31 cubic feet

1 litre = 1·76 imperial pints
1 gram = 15·43 grains = 0·035 ounce
1 kilogram = 2·20 pounds
100 kilograms = 1·97 hundredweights
1 metric ton (tonne) = 2204·6 pounds

direct vertical lift: 1 man = 100 kilograms = 220 pounds
weight on end of lever: 1 man = 50 kilograms = 110 pounds
pull on rope: 1 man = 25 kilograms = 55 pounds

100° Centigrade = 212° Fahrenheit
1000° Centigrade = 1832° Fahrenheit

INTRODUCTION

The term experimental archaeology is a convenient way of describing the collection of facts, theories and fictions that has been assembled through a century of interest in the reconstruction and function of ancient remains. By definition the words suggest a trial, a test, a means of judging a theory or an idea, and this is exactly so; experimental archaeology provides a way, one way, of examining archaeological thoughts about human behaviour in the past. It deals almost entirely with elements of subsistence and technology, and does not therefore encompass the whole range of human culture; yet it treats exactly those ancient features that form the backbone of archaeology as a study, the surviving aspects of material culture. In pursuing these aspects beyond mere recovery and recording, experimental archaeology leads easily and perhaps inevitably into further stages of archaeological work involving more complex and more theoretical models of human patterns of behaviour. These too are experimental, and are constructed and tested in the same ways and with the same aims of the more prosaic 'hardware' models treated in this book.

The use of experiments in archaeology is a logical outcome of the subject itself, man's interest in himself and in his past. It represents no more and no less than a channelling of intelligent curiosity towards an explanation of human behaviour in essentially practical terms. Such curiosity was no doubt present from the beginning, from the time that ancient relics were recognised to be ancient, and experiments with archaeological material began over 150 years ago with the discoveries of the spectacular bronze horns of Scandinavia and the British Isles (p. 163). Contemporary accounts record the enormous success of their finders in attracting the attention of town and country folk alike when they cleared away the peat moss, applied the horns to their mouths, and blew blasts that rivalled Alexander the Great's prodigious horn (range 600 stadia = 69 miles = 111 kilometres). Already, with the first experiments, exaggerated claims were being produced; today these are not so blatantly expressed.

Following the recognition by the scientific world of man's great antiquity, attention was focused upon stone tools recovered from ancient geological deposits, and experimental work was carried out on reproducing and testing flint implements from about 1860. Nilsson, Lubbock, Evans, some of the founders of archaeology, all professed interest in experimenting with stone, and some of Evans's work has never been surpassed. Pitt-Rivers was the first to test ancient digging implements, and to record weathering and silting of the ditches cleared from his excavations. Some experimental work was also done on metals in the later nineteenth century, and on both sides of the Atlantic, serious investigations involving reconstruction work and testing of models were conducted regularly (Ascher 1961, 794; Lynch and Lynch 1968, 57). Well before this time, however, experimental archaeology had suffered its first and only recorded martyr to the subject (p. 165), a gentleman who represents more than anyone the personal hardship endured by many an experimenter working under difficult conditions of all kinds.

The range of experiments that has been conducted over the past 150 years is vast, and this book does not attempt to deal equally with all of it. Some selection has had to be made, but this is based upon an attempt to present a fair picture of experimental archaeology at work in most of its aspects, from mere copies, to faithful reproductions, simple tests, and on to continued series-experiments calculated to yield a range of results. In choosing experiments to describe and assess, personal choice and interest have also figured largely, and some aspects have no doubt been over- or under-represented; for redress, the bibliography will perhaps suffice.

All experiments, or almost all, have common features. All represent problems in archaeological material, through incomplete survival, through loss of understanding of purpose, through doubts about presumed function. All begin with reconstruction, and all go on to tests for function or for suitability. All represent a series of steps: problem → idea → procedure → result → assessment.

The problem can be anything, from forest clearance to the manufacture of ornaments. The idea for a solution can be clear or at least partly vague; one possible answer can be tested, or an experiment run to help decide upon the merits of a variety of possible answers. A multiplier effect applies here: if the action of B and only B upon material A produces an answer Z, then the inference is that B might have been the only method in the past to get Z. However, if Z is also produced by C, and perhaps D as well, then the possibility exists that any one of B, C or D might have been used in the past to get Z. This is perhaps the main source of criticism levelled at experimental archaeology, that it is generally inconclusive. It cannot demonstrate that ancient people did something in a particular way and only in that way; it does not prove anything beyond a shadow of doubt, and this may account for the fact that experimental archaeology tends to be a highly individualistic and generally neglected field. Observations of ancient cultural phenomena are not possible because they have passed without record, but the same difficulty exists for any archaeological exercise that deals with aspects of human behaviour that are not fully represented by material culture.

Confidence in experimental results generally cannot be expressed with precision, and the range of verdicts about the feasibility of a particular method as used in the past tends to include only one specific word 'impossible', and others less dogmatic such as 'unlikely', 'possibly', 'likely', 'probably', presenting an opinion, highly subjective, of the experimenter or commentator on their confidence in the project.

It is important, however, to establish the necessity for some basic procedural rules that are applicable to all experiments, in order that a general measure of reliability can be at least considered if not universally adopted. Most of these rules are observed in most experiments, although they may be unacknowledged as such, because they are basically common sense.

1. The materials used in the experiments should be those considered to have been locally available to the ancient society that produced the problem. An experiment concerned with reproducing prehistoric paintings in southern Africa utilised only those pigments and media obtainable in the immediate vicinity of the sites, and confidence in the results was thereby strengthened (p. 156).

2. The methods used in the experiment to reproduce ancient materials should not exceed those presumed to have been within

the competence of the contemporary society. This presupposes a detailed knowledge of ancient technology, and environment as well, so that measures of expertise can be deduced and accepted. There are two sides to the coin here, because sometimes, in the absence of adequate consideration of ancient technology, experimental work is conducted with 'primitive' tools handled in an inexperienced and therefore inefficient way, and this can reduce the value of the work in an amount equal to the reduction through the use of modern equipment. Digging with antler picks and chopping trees with stone axes are both unaccustomed exercises for modern man (p. 74), and the need for practice before recording efficiency tests is clear.

3. Modern technology should not be allowed to interfere with the experimental results, but should not be neglected in furthering our understanding of the materials and the methods used to alter them. In terms of results, the use of earth-moving machinery to pile up banks and dig ditches may affect the finished products in compaction of material and damage to ditch sides, both demonstrated more than once, and the hauling of replicas of ancient ploughs by tractor can be no substitute for trained paired oxen (p. 33). Yet modern technology provides analyses of materials, such as copper, before, during and after experimental work, and can add beyond measure to our understanding (p. 137).

4. The scope of the experiment should be assessed before work begins. For larger structures, such as Stonehenge, scaled-down models may be adopted (p. 90), but if so then the procedures must be extremely carefully controlled and all elements in the work scaled uniformly. More important is the question of speed in the experiment. Some tests, such as that of rates of erosion and weathering (p. 75), cannot be accelerated by any known means, and patience is ever-virtuous. Other tests, such as building operations (p. 58), can be rapidly completed by modern equipment, but in such cases the experiment suffers through the loss of estimates of time, of observable wear on implements, and perhaps of confidence in the finished product itself. The decision rests with the aim of the project; if a simple copy is needed, of a Celtic chariot (Pl. 1) for example, then modern techniques will doubtless furnish the replica relatively easily. If the rates of time involved in building a wooden house are required, then only methods appropriate to the period in question should be used (p. 55). If rates of decay of a rampart are to be measured (p. 75), then it should be constructed without recourse to agencies likely to misrepresent its compaction and style of building. If a piece of

equipment such as a wooden ard is to be tested, it must be correctly made according to the wood, its grain and its condition, and it must be tried fairly under circumstances assumed to be reasonably close to the original.

5. The experiment should be repetitive if possible, each building on the results of the previous test. The improved and simplified methods of firing pottery in Romano–British kilns were only understood and tried because of earlier attempts (p. 149). The storage of grain in underground pits is another example of the persistence of experiments yielding increasingly useful results (p. 43). In addition, 'it is impossible to profit by a lucky accident unless the mind has been prepared by a long course of thinking and experimenting'.[1]

6. The experimental work will be undertaken with a desired result in mind, but there should exist a genuine uncertainty that the method adopted will succeed, and improvisation should be constantly considered. A variety of procedures should be used if at all possible, to provide a range of possible solutions and prevent blind acceptance of the first successful result. In hardening shields of leather, a number of processes were tried, and the results could then be compared and assessed (p. 146). In a different context, the 'disciplined use of the imagination is the highest function of the archaeologist'.[2]

7. The results of the experiment will consist of a series of observations that lead the archaeologist to certain suggested conclusions. Proof absolute should not be assumed or claimed. Although it is possible to sail an ancient type of boat across the Atlantic (p. 109), the claim that it actually happened in ancient times is not proved. Corroborative evidence is always required to give confidence to experimental results. In the case of notched deer rib-bones, their usefulness in preparing plant fibres for rope-making could be demonstrated, not proved, but subsequent recognition of an ancient notched bone with plant pulp stuck between its teeth supported the likelihood that such tools had served this purpose in ancient times (p. 130).

A field of corroborative evidence that is useful if carefully employed is ethnography. Both experimental archaeology and ethnography will provide ranges of possible solutions to specific problems; neither will prove any particular answer, but both will indicate degrees of probability for the archaeologist to consider. The comparison between iron-smelting furnaces in north-

1. A. M. Hocart, *The Progress of Man* (London, 1933), 49.
2. O. G. S. Crawford, *Archaeology in the Field* (London, 1954), 224.

eastern Africa and in Scandinavia, morphologically similar in appearance, suggests that the processes observed for the former may well have been used for the latter (p. 142).

8. Finally, the experiment should be assessed in terms of its reliability, that it asked the right questions of the material, that the procedure adopted was appropriately conceived and honestly applied, and that the results were observed and assessed fairly. Errors in the experiment, in selection of materials, in processes, in observations, should be openly stated. In working with sheet metal, for example, the use of copper instead of bronze may affect a result (p. 146). And in the final analysis, the reliability of experimentally-derived conclusions must not be assumed. It may be possible to produce fifteen musical notes or noises from a prehistoric horn, but it is not possible, by experiment or any other archaeological procedure, to assert therefore that the landscape of Denmark in about 800 B.C. reverberated to the multifarious notes of these splendid instruments (p. 166).

Experimental archaeology then cannot and does not pretend to prove anything. It provides a tool by which some of the basic economic activities of ancient man, those concerned primarily with subsistence and technology, can be assessed for their development and their competence. As such it can and should lead on to further considerations of patterns of human behaviour, the concern of archaeology as a science and as a humanity.

This book has been arranged in three main sections on the basis of experiments in food production, heavy industry and light industry. Food production tests include forest clearance, ploughing, sowing, harvesting and storing of crops, as well as several dealing with the preparation and consumption of food. Under heavy industry are house building operations, the construction of earthworks and the decay or destruction of both; the transport and erection of stones and monumental buildings are also included, as well as experiments in long distance travel by boat. Light industry, in general the production and testing of smaller portable equipment, concerns craftsmanship in stone, bone, wood, hide, metals and pottery, as well as the arts of painting and music. A short concluding section assesses the value of archaeology by experiment, and makes some suggestions for future consideration and work.

I

FOOD PRODUCTION

FOREST CLEARANCE AND CROPS

The indisputable fact that vast areas of Europe, North America and Asia were forest-covered when the first agriculturists penetrated meant that some procedures had to be immediately introduced to clear the land for cultivation. Although there is increasing evidence that hunter-gatherers had already initiated the process of deforestation through fire, pollen analyses have always shown that there were phases in prehistoric times when forest cover was rapidly depleted, and most of these occur at times when technological advances were particularly marked, or where other pressures must have built up through movement or increase of population. The use of timber in mining activities (for shoring and for smelting), in hill-fort building (for lacing the earthen ramparts and for walling), and in cremating the dead (for funeral pyres) must have depleted a forest cover already decimated in favoured areas by the need for larger and larger tracts of land for cultivation and grazing.

The clearance of forest may be said to represent the first major impact of man upon his environment, as it was the first step leading to a landscape controlled to a great extent by man. The clearance of such forest tracts has always been a subject of some concern to archaeologists and ethnographers who have tried to visualise the ease with which early man coped with his environment. Experiments in this particular subject have ranged from simple functional studies with reconstituted felling-axes, to sequences of work involving not only clearance but cultivation of experimental crops. Some of these have been closely related to pollen and other botanical investigations, in attempts to record the processes of vegetational change in altered areas.

Numbers of experiments concerned with the felling of trees have been conducted; perhaps the first was by the Vicomte Lepic who used a polished flint axe, hafted in an oak root, to chop down an oak tree (Evans 1897, 162). In Denmark, a trial clearance of 2000 square metres of oak forest was made in 1954 (Iversen 1956). Flint axes were used, hafted in accordance with surviving prehistoric hafts, and the trees were felled at knee height. Oaks of greater than 35 cm diameter were not felled but were girdled and left to die, and each of the smaller trees was chopped down in about 30 minutes. A small area of 500 square metres was cleared by 3 men in 4 hours, and from this it was concluded that one man could have cleared ·2 hectare in a week.

A directly comparable experiment was recently carried out in Czechoslovakia in a variety of woods including pine (*Pinus silvestris*), spruce (*Picea excelsa*), alder (*Alnus glutinosa*), birch (*Betula verrucosa*), ash (*Fraxinus excelsior*) and willow (*Salix petraca*). It was found that a small tree, of 14–15 cm diameter, could be felled with a polished stone axe in only 7 minutes (Stelcl and Malina 1970). As in the Danish work, the method of chopping was with the axe held at an angle of about 50 degrees to the trunk of the tree, when a series of short blows would splinter off long chips; the stem of the tree when felled would have a sharpened end, like a pencil, and the stump at knee height would have a smashed top (Pl. 3).

Near Leningrad, an experiment with a polished axe of nephrite found on a Neolithic site showed that a pine of 25 cm diameter could be chopped down in 20 minutes (Semenov 1964, 130), and these figures are comparable to those recorded many years ago by Smith working on hafted flint blades and pinewood (Smith 1893).

Most of the comments made following these experiments have referred to the efficiency of stone axes, and there seems little doubt that such axes on soft woods are almost as effective as metal axes. A direct comparison between stone and steel has been made, however, that purports to show differently (Saraydar and Shimada 1971). A steel axe, weighing 2·3 kg, with a cutting blade 14 cm wide, was compared with a granite axe, 1·8 kg and blade 5 cm wide. The measurement made was of the kilocalories consumed by the manual effort in chopping at 24 strokes per minute for 5 minutes on a 15 cm diameter maple tree. The volume of air expelled was measured and its oxygen content was reckoned, leading to calculations of energy expended. The use of the stone axe consumed 5 times as many kilocalories as did the use of the steel axe, and the conclusion was that the stone axe took 5 times the energy, and 6 times as long, to accomplish the same work as the steel axe. The lack of detail given about precise methods of operation of the axes, and differences in blade thickness, as well as the differing widths and weights of axe, suggest that the work could be repeated with profit.

In the Yukon, recent observations on the felling of spruce trees by chiselling out splinters with wedges or stone axes in a band around the trunk, then pushing the tree over, show that the manner of use of stone axes may not have been that chopping action used by modern man with steel axes. In splintering spruce trees, a contest between stone and steel resulted in a win for the stone axe (Leechman 1950).

The few observations made about the rate of clearance of trees are not particularly useful. The Danish work suggested ·2 hectare of clearance per man per week; in upper Canada in the eighteenth century ·4 hectare could be cleared by one man with a steel axe in a week, the trees felled at knee height, but in a working year a man would rarely clear more than 2 hectares. He would have many other things to do, including burning the land, and it was as important there as in Europe to keep the cleared areas small, with trees around, to allow forest regeneration after land exhaustion. Work in central America has also emphasised these aspects.

If sufficient forethought was given to the process, and if time or energy was a problem, trees to be felled in a few years could be ringed and allowed to die before chopping down. This would have eased the woodchoppers' task. Fire-setting would also have been a method of felling particularly large or hardwood trees. Shaw has recently pointed out that this is an effective procedure for truly enormous trees, and is still in use. In west Africa he observed that a large tree, 44 metres high, was impervious to all efforts with a steel axe that bounced off the hard wood (Shaw 1969). Fire-setting around the base of the previously ringed tree gradually burnt through, and after 60 hours the tree fell as planned by the locals. The effort was estimated as 6 hours of bark stripping, collecting wood and tending the fire. Windrow-felling would also be possible on a slope; the trees would be half chopped through so that when the uppermost trees were finally felled, their fall would knock down the neighbouring trees and so on. It would be a spectacular sight to see the whole hillside cleared at once, although in practice this never occurs completely.

When the efforts of prehistoric man at clearing forest are placed beside those of modern man, the impact of early man appears minute, but in some ways his approach to the problem has hardly been improved. One example must suffice. In the Mato Grosso of Brazil, vast areas of forest are in the process of being cleared so that cattle ranches can be established. The size of some of these ranches beggars the imagination (Fazenda Suia Missu 400000 hectares, Fazenda Dr Paulo 40 × 32 km), and the method of clearance has been described as a mixture of crude destruction and cunning. Using steel axes, men chop down most of the trees, leaving only a few; one man clears ·4 hectare in 10 days. The wood is burnt in the dry month of August, burnt again the next year, and the next, and then coarse grass seed is strewn over the charred remains and tree stumps; the cattle, from zebu stock, are then driven in to graze in this inhospitable area. The scale of the operation is such that nearly 12000 hectares were cleared from one ranch in only 5 years, and 20000 head of cattle established. Beside this, the 1 or 2 hectares of Neolithic man seem puny indeed, but the method of clearance and working of the land is probably identical.

The Danish experiments continued with the burning of half of the cleared area (Steensberg 1955). The brushwood was spread evenly over the ground, and a 10-metre belt was fired, then the burning logs were rolled and pushed forward to the next strip of ground. Care was taken not to burn the ground too heavily, but it had to be heated thoroughly to clear it and to increase its fertility through incorporation of ashes and release of mineral constituents in readiness for the next stage; most clearances of forest involve burning of one sort or another, and controlled experiments have demonstrated the necessity for this in terms of crop yield. Observations on bush fires lasting several days indicate that the soil is heated, and weed roots destroyed, to depths rarely below 20 cm, and a flash fire racing through a lightly wooded area would hardly heat the soil below 7 cm. Clearly, the deliberate clearance of forest for cultivation of crops would necessitate carefully organised and controlled burning of felled timber to prolong the heat and destroy the weed roots.

In the Danish experiment, the area cleared was then hand-sown with wheat and barley. The seed was spread evenly onto the warm ground and raked in with a forked stick. The unburnt but cleared area was also sown in a similar manner. Other experiments in planting have been concerned with the seeding of ploughed ground, and uncertainties have been expressed over the depth of furrow (Reynolds 1967). It has been suggested that to broadcast seed into furrows perhaps 12 cm deep would be wasteful, yet to broadcast onto a ploughed and raked field would only feed a variety of animals, particularly birds. The Roman method of sowing was to broadcast by hand either above furrow or under furrow; seeds sowed onto a flat field would often be ploughed into furrows so that hoeing was possible. Raking would also cover the seeds.

In the Danish experiment, the seed was hand-sown and raked in. Both burnt and unburnt areas were hoed and weeded, and the resulting crops were then compared. The unburnt control area yielded hardly any crop at all, but the burnt area produced a strong crop. In the second year, however, the area's yield was much reduced, and it seems from this that slash-and-burn cultivation of this type was only effective for a very short time before the land lost its fertility. Burning again, the introduction of cattle for manuring, manuring from a farmstead, and fallowing, would all have contributed to the field's regeneration, and no doubt all of these methods were practised; no comparative experiments have been carried out on this vital aspect.

Work in Latin America has provided some confirmation of the results of clearance, burning and successive crops. In one experiment, 10 mecates (c. ·5 hectare) of Yucatan forest was cleared without the use of metal tools (Hester 1953). The vegetation here is dense, with one estimate of between 100 and 200 woody plants per mecate. Wood up to 6 cm diameter was broken by hand, and untreated limestone lumps were used successfully to chop down larger timber except for some trees that were girdled. The stone tools showed no sign of wear after two weeks of work, and would probably have been unrecognisable by archaeologists as anything but natural lumps. The felled wood could have been burnt at almost any time in the year, preferably just after the rainy season, and this would have helped control the grasses, weeds and insects, and furnished ash with mineral salts for the crop.

Another experiment was concerned with the fertility of the soil which tends to be rather thin in much of the southern Maya lowlands (Steggerda 1941). A small experimental plot of one mecate was cleared and planted with corn for 8 successive years. For the first 4 years the field was irregularly weeded, in contemporary native fashion, and the yield by kilogram of shelled corn fell (32–28–16–7); as a control, the same field was weeded regularly for the next 3 years, and the yield was 34–15–24. The competition from weeds was clearly a factor, but more recent work has suggested that soil fertility depletion was probably the major agency in failing crops (Cowgill 1962). That this is, however, not a universal phenomenon has been shown by a lengthy experiment in Colorado (see below).

Observations among surviving groups in the area provide more reliable indications of cultivation procedures and population densities in earlier times. The cycle of shifting slash-and-burn cultivation in use suggests that where a cleared field is planted for one year only, it may be left to regenerate for 1–4 years; if 2 years of crop are obtained then a gap of 3–8 years is likely. Each farmer therefore needs large quantities of land, for both crops and fallow, and one estimate for this area is 1·2–1·6 hectares per person; this leads on to densities of 150–200 per square mile (600–800 per 1000 hectares). Such observations, supported by experimental work, allow much firmer estimates of ancient behaviour patterns in these areas than we can hope to advance in areas where the ethnohistorical material is absent.

An early experiment in the growing of corn was carried out by Franke and Watson in Mesa Verde National Park, Colorado, over a period of years. The report of the experiments after 17 years drew some interesting conclusions (Franke and Watson 1936). In 1918, a small field, one hectare, of heavy red clay soil was chosen near a group of early Pueblo and Basket Maker sites, on the assumption that the same ground was likely to have been cultivated by these ancient settlers under conditions not unlike those of today; in these, rainfall was and is of extreme importance. The average annual fall from 1908–20 was 43 cm, varying from a drought of 25 to 56 cm; the fall occurs twice, February–March and July–December, and the driest season is June when the crops are at risk.

The field was cleared of brushwood, and fenced against animals and humans. Each year it was ploughed and planted in early May by Navajo Indians; the main crop was of calico corn or squaw corn, but beans and squash were also grown. The planting method was that used by the Navajos on their own farms. A hole about 38 cm wide and 13 cm deep is dug, and a smaller hole then dug in the base; the seed corn, 10–12 seeds, is dropped in and buried by soil filling only the small hole. When the young shoots emerge, they spread upwards and it is not until they reach the ground surface that the larger hole is filled in. The purpose of this method is to obtain deeper supplies of moisture for the seed. The small hills of earth that result from this process are 1–2 metres apart, and hoeing is done twice in the summer. Manuring of the field only occurred twice in 17 years.

In the early part of the experiment, planting sticks were used by the older Indians and 'a prayer was tamped into every hill'. In later years, shovels were used by younger Indians, and the prayers were neglected. The absence of prayer had no noticeable effect on the yield, another interesting experiment.

Each year, germination tests of the crop were carried out, and in only 2 years out of the original 17 was crop failure drastic. In both cases, drought was the sole cause; the extremely dry spring months did not allow the soil to hold enough water to support the young crop until the summer rains arrived. In all the other years the crop was successful, sometimes more so than others.

No measurements were made of the actual yield of corn, as birds and rodents depleted the field, and Indian tracks to the nearest village also suggested that some of the experimental crop was being experimentally consumed. The surviving ears, however, were far larger than those from the ancient settlements nearby. There is some evidence to suggest that the abandonment of the Mesa Verde area was because of continued drought, and if so then the comparison between the latest corn cobs from the settlement and those grown under better conditions is not significant in terms of cultivation practices.

The other crops experimentally grown, beans and squash, fared differently. The bean shoots were regularly consumed by rabbits and squirrels. The squash, as well as occasional cantaloupes, watermelons and potatoes, were successfully grown. The advantage of growing beans in the same field, a practice in current use, is that beans add nitrogen to the soil, and it is this element that corn exhausts. Alternate growing of beans and corn is a useful method of rotation. The small hills where corn had grown the previous year also help to maintain the fertility of the soil; planting each year is done in positions beside the surviving hills, not in exactly the same spot, and in this way soil depletion is avoided. The results after the first 17 years of experiments were impressive. Good crops were still being produced annually, and the latest crops were as successful as the first. In the same area, tests showed that soil depletion had not occurred after 30 years continuous crops in particular situations, yet within 2 or 3 km only 2 years' crop could be obtained before manuring or resting the land. Some soils, of dry and sandy types, are far less able to maintain their fertility than others obtaining identical amounts of rainfall.

In the Old World, observations on shifting cultivation or slash-and-burn farming as practised by recent communities in Russia are particularly relevant to the Danish experiments (Linnard 1970). The stages in this practice began with careful site selection, taking into account opportunities for hunting in the adjacent areas and the types of trees growing. Alder woods were preferred as they yielded more wood-ash than most trees; birch and spruce woods were also suitable, but pine was avoided. The size of trees was not as important as the types of trees, as the latter were used as soil indicators.

With rather primitive tools, the peasants preferred to kill the trees by girdling them or removing the bark; in this way the trees took from 5 to 15 years to die. Some areas, however, were cleared by direct axe-felling, carefully done so that the ground was uniformly covered by wood. Felling was done in June, in a season free of agricultural work, with a drying summer ahead. Felled trees took 1 to 3 years to dry, girdled trees were dried before the trees actually toppled.

Burning was done against the wind so that the process was slow and more thorough, to destroy surface roots down to about 5 cm. Re-burning was carried out on patches not burned by the first conflagration. The seed was then sown straight into the warm ash with or without tilling the soil. A spruce tree top was used to harrow the ground, cover the seed and loosen weeds.

In many areas of north Russia, only one crop was taken from the new land, but often 2 or 3 crops were attempted. The yields dropped dramatically after the first year, and, when abandoned, the area was generally left for 20 to 40 years. These observations conform almost exactly to the conclusions reached by the experimental clearance work.

One by-product of the type of experimental work that was conducted in Denmark on the slash-and-burn method of cultivation was the observation that the weeds returning to the cleared area differed remarkably between the unburnt and the burnt portions. The unburnt control gradually was invaded again by bracken, sedges and grasses, almost the same types as had existed there before clearance, but more luxuriant now that more sunlight penetrated through to them. The burnt area, however, was soon colonised by entirely new plants, plantain, dandelion, daisies, and thistles, precisely the types that are associated in pollen diagrams throughout north-western Europe with decline in tree pollen at various stages in prehistory. As trees such as elm decrease in the pollen record, these weeds of cultivation increase, and they must mark phases of exploitation by early agriculturists. No experiments with the feeding of elm shoots to cattle, one of the presumed reasons for the sudden elm decline, have been made; the introduction of sheep in parts of Europe no doubt also contributed to this decline, as they tend to ring elm trees by eating the bark.

Records were also made of the trees that gradually encroached upon the cleared areas. Birch seedlings and willow saplings appeared, and shoots of hazel, aspen and lime soon grew up from roots that had survived the burning. Mosses were also soon in evidence on the burnt ground. The representation of these trees in pollen diagrams often shows enormous quantities of hazel; hazel produces much more, and more resistant, pollen than some associated plants, but its over-representation in pollen profiles may also be due to animal preferences. The introduction of cattle upon the unburnt field in the Danish experiment, to see how they reacted upon the vegetation, clearly showed that hazel was avoided by the animals and its representation in the pollen record was that much more enlarged. The cattle would of course help maintain the fertility of the field; in the Brazilian clearances, the cattle are expected to help maintain an already rich ground without other fertilisers for at least 20 years.

PLOUGHING

Any attempts to understand the processes of early agricultural activities are hampered as much by the extreme rarity of ancient implements as by the scarcity of the marks of their use on soils long since altered by modern man. Yet the production of food in estimable quantities through an awareness of the potentialities of seeds and soils was one of the human actions that led on to forms of settled life and the development of many of the practices that we term civilisation. For archaeologists searching for the traces of early agricultural activities, the recovery of an ard, or the recognition of plough marks in sealed soils, generally represents an important advance in our knowledge of the methods of food production. Traces of cultivation furrows have been increasingly recognised in recent years both in the British Isles and on the continent, but the implements themselves have rarely survived (Fig. 1). The importance of experiments with replicas of ards lies not only in the replication of the implements, but in the traces of wear upon them and in the field markings that remain after they

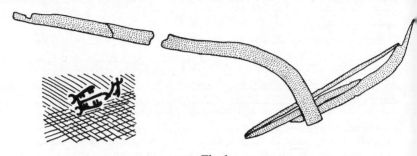

Fig. 1

The Donnerupland ard; length of foreshare 1·3 m. Cross-ploughing marks and rock art representation of a plough team

have been tested. Of the major ploughing experiments that have been carried out in Europe, that conducted in Denmark is without doubt the most ambitious and most rewarding.

In 1957 a wooden ard was recovered from a peatbog at Hendriksmose in Jutland; it was radiocarbon dated to 350 B.C. ± 100, and the wood identified as oak. The ard was treated to prevent decay and was then available for study; it is possible that some distortion occurred during preservation, but this was not considered to have seriously affected the performance of the replicas that were made in 1962 and 1968 (Hansen 1968, 1969).

The Hendriksmose ard is of a type described as a 'bow-ard with passing-through stilt' (Glob 1951). It consists of a curved one-piece stilt and ard-head that passes through the beam (Fig. 2a). On top of the ard-head lies a stout wooden bar-share. There are notches at the head of the beam (for the yoke), a single notch in the ard-head behind the beam-hole, and a perforation at the top of the stilt (for a handle); the notch in the ard-head is of crucial importance, and may have held a wedge which would have tightened and spread the pressure from the ard-head and share onto the upper and lower surfaces of the hole in the beam.

The first replica was made of this simple ard in 1962 and was tested in 1967 and 1968 at the Research Centre, Lejre (Hansen 1969). Two other copies were produced in 1968, one by a carpenter and one by someone who was to use the ard in ploughing.

Because of difficulties in obtaining suitable materials for these replicas some divergencies in the shape of the ards had to be accepted; the problems lay in the sharply-curved stilt as well as in the curved beam.

Before ploughing experiments could be carried out with these ards, a pair of oxen had to be found that would fit the ard and operate as a trained team; most rock engravings of plough scenes of the Bronze Age and later periods in Europe, principally in northern Italy but also in Scandinavia, show paired oxen (Fig. 1). In 1965 two Jersey bull calves were obtained by the Research Centre and later castrated. The aim was to obtain strong animals of low shoulder heights, to match estimates of the size of Iron Age bulls with shoulder heights of 130 cm. The pair eventually selected had relevant heights of 147 and 133 cm.

These heights do not represent the point of draught, however, because the yoke attached to the beam does not rest upon the shoulders but lower down on the back of the animals' heads; the beam is also slung beneath the yoke so that the point of draught can be 20 cm below the shoulder height (Fig. 2d). In use, though, the yoke drags the horns of the animals backwards, thus raising the heads and necks by up to 10 cm and the point of draught by an equal amount. All of this is important for the angle of use of the ard, and partly determines whether or not it penetrates the ground evenly.

The training of the oxen was carried out by an initial period of harnessing the beasts to a log which was dragged about. This is standard practice and was also used in the training of ponies for chariotry in Britain (Pl. 1) The oxen were trained irregularly for about 6 weeks, with the intention of enabling them to walk together at a uniform and slow pace for long periods; it was also hoped to train them to turn at the end of a furrow, and to proceed on a course parallel to the previous furrow. The last two requirements were not met by this team, and three helpers were eventually enlisted to guide the oxen, one helper on each side and a third to encourage the oxen to pull harder when they showed signs of flagging (Pl. 2). The director of the experiment suggests that it would have been cheaper to buy fully-grown oxen and to train them intensively, rather than develop a team from the calf stage.

The fields selected for ploughing at Skamlebaek in northern Zealand were light and sandy. The experiments here were designed to study the capabilities of the ard in breaking up a developed fallow ground as well as the ard traces in more easily ploughed

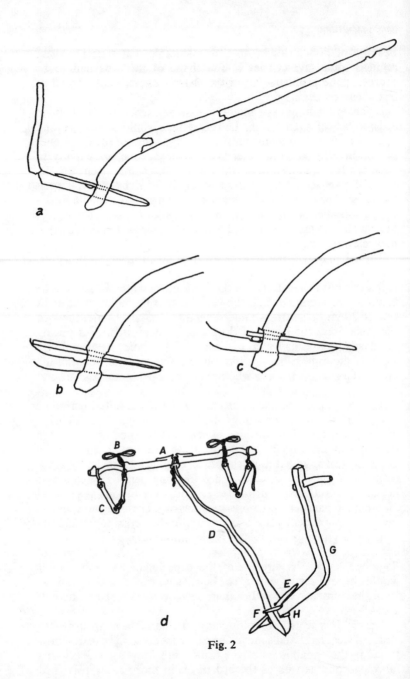

Fig. 2

subsoils. The first field had lain fallow for 30 years, and various plots were laid out to allow

single ≡ criss-cross ⧣ and diagonal-cross ⧦ ploughing. The long grass was cut and removed before the ploughing attempts were made. The second field had been cultivated eighteen months before, and some of the top soil was removed so that the ard would pass easily through the light sands. In both sets of experiments, the oxen, the ard, the helpers and the soils were recorded and measured so that as complete a series of observations were collected as possible; these mainly related to certain questions that were asked of the work, questions about time and energy for oxen and helpers, wear for the ard, and ploughmarks for the fields.

One of the first problems concerned the necessity for a wooden wedge in the notch on the upper surface of the stilt (ard-head). Without this, the bar-share slid back and was pressed against the stilt curve (Fig. 2b), and could not cut into the soil unless almost all of the grass had been removed. The point of the share was too close to the end of the ard-head, and it was not until a wedge was introduced that the share was held firmly forward of the ard-head by about 10 cm. Most published illustrations of ards of this type are shown with the share in the wrong position (e.g., Fig. 1). Various experiments were carried out with wedges in different positions so that the share angle varied; this is the angle between the line of the share and the bottom of the furrow, and about 35–38° was found to be the most satisfactory for this particular ard; a wedge was necessary so that the bar-share should protrude by 10 cm (Fig. 2c). In this situation the ard could break up eighteen-month grass or light fallow ground.

A second observation on the ploughing experiments concerned the speed and power of the oxen. Measurements of the draught power were particularly useful, as it showed clearly that the oxen could pull little more than 200 kg. In ploughing the developed fallow ground, the oxen moved forward steadily at a loading of about 100 kg, but when the ard dug more deeply into the soil the load increased to 150 kg and the oxen slowed; when the share

Fig. 2

a The wooden ard from Hendriksmose, Denmark (1/20)
b Share slip without wedge
c Share position with wedge
d Replica prepared for use: A, yoke with neck ties C and horn loops B; D, beam with bar-share E; tightening key F for stilt G and E; H, back wedge

(after Hansen 1969)

dipped down or got held back by thick turf, the load was increased suddenly to 200 kg and this more or less stopped the team. A second ploughing of the same field, deepening the furrows, resulted in average loads of 100 kg and there was no trouble over the team. These observations are important as they can be used in making estimates of the amount of labour, size of teams, and even type of ards, that would be necessary in working stiff soils or fallow ground in other regions. The plough marks recovered from prehistoric sites, or evidence from pollen or soils in an area, are two sources of such information that could be linked with these ploughing experiments.

One of the major difficulties encountered in the ploughing was the inability of the replica ard to cut through the turf of old fallow ground. The share would slide or jump on the grass, sometimes digging in but rarely maintaining contact with the soil. Reduction of the share angle, and sharpening of the wooden point, made some improvement but the ard would only cut through the turf for about one metre before running up and out again. The experiments on old fallow ground were abandoned at this point, but it is possible that hoeing or burning could have loosened the soil before ploughing, or that an arrow-shaped, ristle, share, documented from various parts of Europe, would have sliced through the grass before the normal bar-share was tried.

A large series of observations was made on the traces of ploughing that remained in the light sandy subsoils of a field which had been pared of topsoil. Areas were ploughed and then excavated, both horizontally and vertically. One of the quite remarkable discoveries from this was that almost all of the traces in the soil did not correspond at all with the shape of the share. They were much wider than the share, and tended to be rounded in cross-section rather than angular. Arrow-shaped shares, however, did leave angular traces. Soil also tended to be dragged along, so that darker topsoil would fill the upper part of the trace, while lighter subsoil would fill the lower part. With weathering and erosion it is difficult to see how such marks would be recognisable as plough traces, although in some cases it seems that subsoil particles were dragged into the topsoil trace. The dragging zone, however, was found to be useful in determining the sequence of plough furrows in fields where cross-ploughing had occurred, as the later trace would chop through and bend the earlier trace. Much more information about plough traces of the Iron Age has recently come to light (e.g., Nielsen 1970) and can be compared directly with the experimental record.

Finally the bar-share and ard-head were examined regularly for signs of abrasion and wear. Such wear would differ markedly between light sandy soils and stony soils. On gravel and loam in a stubble field, about ·5 kilometre of ploughing reduced an oak share by 15–18 mm. Resharpening of the share in the most economical way possible, after a dozen furrows, would reduce it by 3 mm. On these figures, the Hendriksmose ard would have needed 6 bar-shares to plough ·5 hectare. The original share, by its condition, appears to have been practically, but not entirely, new when it was deposited in the peatbog.

This work marks a significant advance on our knowledge of ancient ploughing implements. In Czechoslovakia, experiments on ploughs and ards of the eighteenth century were carried out in 1946–7, using teams of horses. In England, experiments with a reconstructed ard based on a find at Donnerupland, Denmark (Fig. 1), were conducted in 1956–7, and observations were made about cross-ploughing and the turning of furrows; the experiments were hampered by the lack of a trained team of oxen, a single horse and then a tractor being used (Aberg and Bowen 1960). The ard itself was made in the Museum of English Rural Life at Reading. It was rather more complex than the Hendriksmose ard, although of the same general type, consisting of a curved beam with a slot through which passes an arrow-shaped share carrying a foreshare, the whole resting upon the ard-beam part of the stilt. There are parts of comparable ards known from Scottish peatbogs (Fenton 1962–3). Recently, another copy of the Donnerupland ard was made and tested (Reynolds 1967); this was not a close copy but was basically the same type, and it proved successful in ploughing light soils at Bredon in Gloucestershire when pulled by students.

None of these experiments, however, would claim to have been as exhaustive or extensive as those with the Hendriksmose replicas, and there are several lessons to be learned from this experimental series. The importance of accurate recording of ards as soon as they are found, and before conservation processing, is paramount; some of the difficulties with the replicas of this ard may have been due to the making of copies based on an altered original. The team of oxen must be trained over a long period so that it functions at a standard pace and pull, and does not add to the experimental problems which are varied enough as it is. These other problems—the share angle, the presumed necessity of a wedge, the dificulties with old fallow ground, and the ard marks in the soil—can only be resolved by further experimental work along with more studies of ancient implements and ethnographic observations. Taken together, these lines of enquiry should allow us to make much more accurate estimates of the efficiency of prehistoric cultivation methods, which could then be related to the increasing evidence, through pollen and soil studies, of forest clearance and land utilisation on massive scales at various periods in prehistory.

HARVESTING

One of the earliest experiments in the harvesting of crops was carried out in 1937-9 at Lyngby in Denmark, under the direction of Axel Steensberg. Harvesting implements of flint had been the subject of much conjecture since the recognition that some flint sickles had a gloss clearly visible on their edges. Spurrell in 1892 had gone so far as to make a copy of a sickle and to use it to saw bone, wood and horn, and to cut ripe straw; only the straw left a gloss on the ridges and hollows of the flint edge (Spurrell 1892). Curwen, in a series of papers on ancient agricultural practices, also showed that the reaping of siliceous grasses and corn produced a high gloss on flints, and that other forms of polish were caused by the sawing and chopping of wood (Curwen 1930a). The work of Steensberg accepted this result but carried the experiments into an entirely different line of approach. His work represents an important first stage in any consideration of harvesting in ancient times, as it is concerned with the basic reaping tools and their efficiency (Steensberg 1943).

Copies were made of flint, bronze and iron sickles such as had been recovered from prehistoric contexts in northern Europe. These tools included a straight-edged flint blade without secondary retouch, a curved flint blade without retouch, a flint with a serrated edge, bronze sickles with smooth and serrated edges, modern iron sickles and Viking and Roman iron scythes. All of these were hafted in accordance with prehistoric handles that had survived in water-logged deposits (Fig. 3).

Two series of experiments were carried out with these implements, the first at Lyngby on a clay soil that had produced 8 plots of drill-sown barley mixed with 18 per cent oats. The 8 plots, each of 50 square metres, were selected to be equally well served by light, drainage and soil type. The crops were sampled before the harvesting operation to ensure that the quantity of straws to be cut by the implements was more or less uniform; in fact, some plots were found to contain up to 20 per cent more straws than

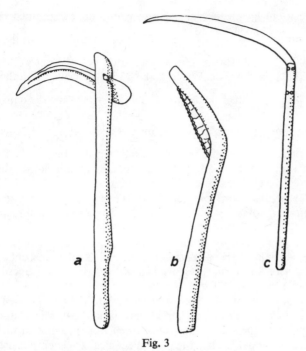

Fig. 3

Harvesting implements (after Steensberg 1943)
a Bronze Age sickle of bronze
b Flint with serrated edge
c Viking scythe of iron

others, and adjustments to the hard figures recorded were then made.

The procedure adopted is perhaps best explained by reference to one of the experiments, using a bronze sickle with crescentic serrated edge on Steensberg's plot number 3. As one bunch of corn was grasped, it was cut as efficiently as possible with the sickle; a second bunch was then held and cut and so on, until five bunches formed a handful, beyond which it was not convenient to hold and cut; in 58 minutes it was possible to clear the plot by cutting 331 handfuls. There is little comment in the report on the efficiency or experience of the operator which would of course be crucial in this experiment. From the 331 handfuls, 20 were selected and their composition was recorded. These contained 1130 barley straws, of which 54 had been uprooted and not cut by the sickle, and 143 oat straws, with 4 uprooted; 18 weeds had also been cut by the sickle. The plot would have contained 18 702 barley straws $\left(\dfrac{331 \times 1130}{20}\right)$ plus 2367 oat straws, the total therefore being 21 069 straws. The average number of straws for each of the plots used was reckoned to be 26 646, so that the index for plot 3 with its bronze sickle was 89·1 $\left(\dfrac{21\,069}{26\,646}\right)$; thus the equalised reaping time for this plot was 65 minutes $\left(\dfrac{58 \times 100}{89\cdot1}\right)$. In this way it was possible to obtain consistent and comparable results for all of the implements used in the experiments, and some idea of their relative efficiencies could be gained.

Observations were also made on the procedure for handling each implement when cutting the straws. Some, the crescentic bronze sickle for instance, were most effective when held low, at ground level, and then pulled upwards onto the bunch of straws, leaving stubble 15–17 cm high. Others, such as the crescentic flint blade, cut best in a more vigorous and horizontal movement in a half circle around the straws; the stubble length was 12–20 cm. Recent observations in Iran and in Calabria have pointed out various tricks employed by hand harvesters in gathering handfuls of corn for the sickle, in bunching these together and in moving them from the field. The role played by gleaners is emphasised in both accounts (Lerche 1968; Rasmussen 1969).

A second series of experiments with some of the same, and some other, sickles was held on a sandy loam with a crop of hand-sown barley mixed with 3·1 per cent oats. The straw count varied by about 12 per cent within the 8 plots. Two iron scythes were included in the tools, and were employed as two-handed implements so that the bunch technique for handfuls was not used; both were extremely efficient in cutting through the straws, but tended to scatter the corn. It is likely they were used for grasses and reeds rather than corn crops.

The results of the experiments can be combined into a table that sets out the functional efficiency of all the tools tested. The table shows the percentage of uprooted straws for each implement, the actual and equalised reaping time, and the number of bunches (cuts) for each handful. The uprooted percentages reflect the sharpness and manipulation of the tools, as well as the efficiency and experience of the operators, which we must take as uniform throughout the series in the absence of conflicting evidence. This index is probably an important one, as uprooted and therefore earthy straws would have been avoided if possible by farmers

EXPERIMENTS WITH STONE, BRONZE AND IRON SICKLES AND SCYTHES

Experiment No.	Implement	Material	Uprooted straws as % of total		Reaping time		Cuts per handful
			Barley	Oats	Equalised	Actual	
II.8	Viking scythe	iron	0	0	—	17	—
II.7	Roman Iron Age scythe	iron	0	0	—	30	—
I.1	Galician sickle	iron	0·4	0	30	26	3
I.2	Slovakian sickle	iron	1·7	0	31	32	3
II.6	unhafted straight-edge	flint	0·7	0	72	70	8
II.2	knob sickle, smooth-edge	bronze	1·9	0	60	57	7
I.8			2·1	2·0	64	69	5
II.1	sickle, serrated edge	bronze	2·6	0	66	65	5
I.3			4·7	2·8	65	58	5
I.4	crescentic, smooth-edge	flint	4·0	3·6	59	60	8
II.3			4·4	0	68	73	8
II.5	unhafted straight-edge	flint	6·2	0	90	90	8
II.4	Stenhild straight-edge	flint	2·7	7·7	101	104	8
I.5			11·5	6·7	76	80	8
I.6	crescentic, serrated edge	flint	6·5	7·9	73	81	10

concerned with processing, use and storage of the crops. The equalised reaping time is a less certain index of importance, as our knowledge of ancient man's concern about the passage of time is practically nil. We might assume that he would have been as interested as ourselves in getting a job done when it had to be done. The third index, cuts per handful, is not as relevant to the efficiency of the sickle blades as to the manner in which they were hafted and held.

The table shows some obvious and some surprising facts. The availability of iron as a material for the production of cutting edges was clearly of great importance to early man. The Viking and Roman Iron Age scythes cut through everything, and wasted little time in doing so, but their probable use on grasses and reeds, instead of corn, has been noted. The modern iron sickles were almost as effective as the scythes for cutting corn, and were more efficient than any other sickles. The logical regression, iron to bronze to flint, in the production of cutting edges is interrupted here, however, by the surprising result of the flint blade with un-retouched straight edge. This was used without a handle, and was extremely sharp and effective as a cutter, if very slow in use; the time taken to clear the plot is a clear reflection of the difficulty in use, where eight bunches had to be separately cut to make one handful. More recent trials with flint sickles have also emphasised their functional efficiency (Reynolds 1967). The bronze sickles require little comment, and most of the flint blades seemed to the experimenters to lie near the bottom of the table.

The flint used in experiment II.4 and I.5 was a copy of a straight-edged blade mounted at a right angle in a wooden haft, the implement based closely on a complete tool found at Stenhild. In practice the sickle cut best high above the ground, the blade turned obliquely upwards and moving to the right so that it could meet the straws as they were drawn over to the left by the hand. This was both slow and tiring work. It was concluded that this implement was too inefficient as a sickle, and was probably a weeding hook, too fragile for cutting twigs and leaves but suitable for clearing plots of ground of weeds such as thistles. Similarly, the crescentic flint with serrated edge was less effective than the straight-edged flint; the crescent shape was clearly desired by ancient man and it was therefore probably not a sickle but a saw or leaf knife.

The principal result of the experiments in terms of ancient harvesting implements was the relatively high degree of success obtained by flint when compared with metals, particularly bronze, but another result surely is the recognition that an experiment of this kind when carried out as objectively as possible can yield other data; these may be taken here to include the recognition of the existence of the weeding hook and the leaf knife as ancient implements, and the assertion yet again that unshaped (unretouched) flint blades or flakes could have served as tools throughout prehistory, their lack of archaeologically distinguishable marks being no hindrance to their efficiency.

STORAGE OF FOOD

The storage of food produce has been a source of archaeological concern for many years, ever since Pitt-Rivers suggested that deep pits in Cranborne Chase had been used to store food (Pitt-Rivers 1887, 12–13). The successful preservation of food for future use must have always taxed prehistoric man, and the achievement of methods whereby grain could be kept in storage for consumption and planting must have opened a range of possibilities to man that profoundly affected his existence. The status of a human group, the organisation of its economy, the size of population, all depend to a certain extent on its success in planned food utilisation, and in this, storage is of paramount importance.

The impetus leading to actual experiments in the storage of food was the excavation of the Iron Age settlement at Little Woodbury, Wiltshire (Bersu 1940). At this site, many deep pits were exposed; the capacity of each was 1·5–2 cubic metres and they either were cylindrical or had narrow necks and wider bases, beehive-like. Most other pits believed to have been used for storage on chalk are of these shapes (Fig. 4c), and pits on gravel sites are necessarily cylindrical.

In many areas of the world, pits like these are used for storing various vegetable crops. Some Iron Age sites in Rhodesia and Zambia have contained small numbers of beehive pits, 50–70 cm diameter and 70–100 cm deep; one site, the Khami Waterworks, had larger pits containing domestic debris and quantities of seeds of *Mabela* or Kaffircorn (*Sorghum caffrorum*) (Cooke 1953). Modern villages in the same area employ similar pits for storage, and these are sometimes very large and dug inside the cattle kraal; the walls are plastered with termite mound material which is then hardened by a fire inside the pit. *Mabela* is poured in, and the opening is sealed by stone slabs and termite mound, with cattle dung on top. The heat of the manure, and the movement of cattle over the pit, helps the preservation of the grain and prevents damp

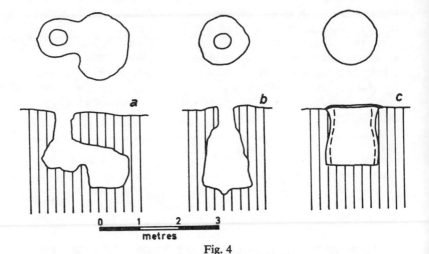

Fig. 4

Plans and sections of storage pits
a,b *Chultuns* in limestone at Tikal, Guatemala (after Puleston 1971)
c   Pit in chalk with basketry lining and lid at Broad Chalke, Wiltshire
     (after Bowen and Wood 1968)

from entering. Pests are excluded by the lining, and the grain will apparently keep for years (Robinson 1963). The practice of piling manure and debris over the pit to seal it might well lead to the collapse of such deposits when the pit was opened. The resulting fill would be comparable to that recovered from many pits on many prehistoric sites.

Although Classical authors describe the storage of grain in Mediterranean lands, these comments cannot really be applied to northern areas where climatic conditions are so different; the Germans, however, are recorded as storing food in cavities dug in the ground, and piling refuse on top to disguise them. Bell-shaped pits dug into the rock in Guatemala and the Mexican highlands have also been demonstrated to be food storage pits. Centuries before, storage vessels at Troy were buried underground and covered by lids so that they could be walked over.

The range of examples of underground storage facilities could be extended, but it seems apparent that grain could be preserved beneath ground in a variety of situations, all of which, however, involved sealing the pits in some substantial way. This is the basis for the experimental work carried out on grain storage both in Britain and abroad.

In Guatemala, pits of considerable size dug into limestone have often been interpreted, correctly, as water cisterns. Some of these *chultuns* have masonry walls and vaulting, and plaster lining. The experimental replastering of a *chultun*, which then filled with rainwater, demonstrated its function, and others have been restored and used as water supplies (Blom 1936).

In the southern Maya lowlands, however, the *chultuns* are different, and instead of a deep bottle-shaped chamber (Fig. 4*b*), they often have small side-chambers reached from a shallow ante-chamber. These pits were originally considered to be for food storage, but this idea was subsequently submerged by the water cistern theory adduced from the much larger and differently shaped *chultuns* of northern Yucatan. The southern lowland pits, however, lack plastered walls and are often found in situations above rainwater catchment areas. The theory of food storage was therefore reasserted, and to this was added other functions: burial chambers, weaving chambers, sweat baths, marl mines, refuse pits, latrines, and non-functional palm tree root-holes. Because of this array, experiments were carried out at Tikal to determine the function of the side-chambered *chultuns* (Puleston 1971).

Of 60 excavated *chultuns* at this site, over 80 per cent have side-chambers (Fig. 4*a*). They occur throughout the residential area, often on higher ground, with stone lids, and many have a raised sill between the ante-chamber and the side-chamber. The theory of water storage was eliminated by experiment, as water poured in drained away through the porous limestone. All the other explanations were discarded on the grounds of lack of sup-porting evidence, until the food storage theory remained to be tested.

A *chultun* was excavated (p. 74) through the hard limestone capping and into the softer marl. Various vegetables were gathered, including maize, beans, squash and sweet potato. Control samples were stored above ground, and the main sample in the *chultun*. All were examined about every 2 weeks for 11 weeks. Most of the *chultun* food was ruined by damp, and much of the above-ground material had been eaten or decayed. The *chultun* provided protec-tion from vermin, but did not function well as storage for grain or root crops, principally because of the high humidity (about 100 per cent). Maize today is stored in the area in dry well-ventilated conditions. A further test, with parched maize, was also disastrous.

In 1967, however, the high nutritional value of the ramon seed (*Brosimum alicastrum*, a tree), and its distributional correlation with Maya sites, suggested that this may have been a major element in Maya food. Ramon seeds were experimentally stored in the *chultun* in 1968, and emerged after 9 weeks in immaculate condition. After 13 months of storage they remained completely edible although their basketry containers had decomposed. The explanation for this survival is probably in the low water content of ramon seeds, 6·5 per cent, which even in a humidity of 100 per cent does not rise to a level that will support fungus action. The result of this experiment has been support for the idea of Mayan ramon cultivation, as well as for the interpretation of the *chultuns* as storage pits for this one type of food.

In Britain, there has been considerable activity in experimentation with storage pits in chalk, clay, gravel and marl. Some of the first studies were arranged by the Ancient Fields (now Ancient Agriculture) Research Committee of the British Association for the Advancement of Science and the Council for British Archaeology (Bowen and Wood 1968). The earliest experiment was devised as a trial run, to see if further work was possible and desirable. Pits were to be dug in chalk, basketry linings inserted, modern threshed corn dumped in and the pits sealed against the English winter at Broad Chalke, Wiltshire. The experiments were carried out over the winters of 1964–5 and 1965–6, and 4 pits were dug; 2 of these were large, 1·4 metres deep and 1·2 metres wide (Fig. 4c), the others were smaller.

The first discovery to be made in this experiment was that the amount of grain the large pits would hold had been grossly underestimated by Bersu (1940); the factor of error was 9. An average large pit, with a volume of 1·6 cubic metres, would hold 44 bushels of barley, not 5 bushels. This mistake in calculation was not discovered experimentally, but had survived for 25 years before estimates of the quantity of barley needed for the experiment were worked out and the error brought to light. The consequences for estimation of acreage and population in Iron Age Britain are considerable.

The pits were dug out with modern pick and shovel, and lined with basketry. The two large pits had a basketry strip inserted, as the weaver considered it impossible to make a continuous circlet inside the pits and such a shape could not have been inserted from the top of the beehive-like pit. The strips were 5 metres long and 1·5 metres wide, and took 18 hours to weave. The fact that this clearly was a major time element in the use of pits for storage was considered to contribute to the few traces of basketry in ancient pits, and it was believed that the strips would have been withdrawn for repair and use elsewhere as they were so expensive to make. These ideas are perhaps not so likely now that the lining of pits has been shown not to be necessary (see below).

The pits were left to air for 2 months, then given a straw flooring and filled with modern grain at between 18 and 14 per cent moisture content. Copper pipes were let in at depths of 50 and 100 cm to allow aspiration of carbon dioxide. Grain respires and uses up oxygen, giving off carbon dioxide in the process. If the container of the grain is sealed, the grain will respire until the oxygen is used up, and the grain will then become more or less dormant. The amount of heat available is also relevant, and in most experiments the carbon dioxide readings are plotted along with ground temperatures.

The pits were sealed by wooden lids packed with clay, protected by asbestos sheeting with chalk rubble on top. The experimental nature of this study, designed to show if proper sealing would preserve the grain, dictated that all available means be adopted, and this included the asbestos. The pits were left over a mild winter, and then opened. Field mice had broken the seal on one pit and some water had entered, but over 50 per cent of the grain at the sides, and 90 per cent of the central grain, germinated after 4 days. The second large pit had retained its seal, and 96 per cent germination occurred after 7 days. One of the small pits had been covered but unsealed, and the grain had sprouted and failed.

Later experiments with grain storage pits have built upon these trial results. At Bredon Hill, Gloucestershire, pits were dug in an attempt to answer several questions relating to comparative storage of wet and dry grain, comparative use of lined and unlined pits, the feasibility of opening a pit for partial grain removal and resealing, and the possible storage of grain in the ear. The deposits in which the pits were dug consisted of upper sandy loam and lower limestone bedrock (Reynolds 1967).

Two pits were lined with cylindrical baskets, and the bottoms covered by 45 cm of straw. Barley was poured in to surface level, 840 kg at 22 per cent moisture content in one pit, and 990 kg at 14 per cent in the other pit. Copper tubes were put in place, at 38 and 91 cm depths, with glass taps at the top for aspiration tests. A wooden lid covered with a moist clay dome sealed the wet pit and rubble was then piled on top; the dry pit was sealed with clay bonded directly onto the grain, topped with a limestone rubble dome.

After six months, the pits were opened, and although the dry grain from the larger pit was almost totally recovered in good condition, the side wall of the other pit had partly collapsed and had allowed water to seep in, seriously affecting the grain. The CO_2 readings taken at intervals had already suggested that difficulties had occurred. The normal CO_2 concentration was ·0006 gm/litre, ·03 by volume per cent, and the readings from the dry pit had been consistently higher than those from the unsuccessful pit: dry pit 2–4 per cent, other pit below 1 per cent. These CO_2 readings correlated quite well with the ground temperatures, and it appears that an increase in temperature increases the rate of respiration which accelerates the production of CO_2. The grain from the dry pit was edible and had 67 per cent germination; half of the grain from the other pit was edible but none germinated.

A smaller pit, lined with straw at the bottom and holding 152 kg of grain, was sealed with a reed lid caulked with clay and piled with soil and clay. No basketry or other lining was provided. After 4 months the pit was opened and large samples of grain removed; the pit was then resealed. After a further 2 months the pit was opened again, and it was found that most of it was excellently preserved, with a germination rate of 60 per cent. The grain at the sides of the pit had stuck to the sandy loam wall to a depth of 5 cm, providing a grain-wall.

A fourth pit, lined with basketry, was used to store grain in the ear, and this was successful, with 70 per cent germination. The space required in a storage pit for grain in the ear is 1·6 times that needed for threshed grain.

Further series of experiments with storage pits in sandy loam, clay, gravel and marl have confirmed these results although difficulties have been encountered through vermin breaking the seals and by winter flooding in clay (Reynolds 1969, 1972). It has yet to be determined if and why grain storage pits have gone sour or have been abandoned in prehistoric times, and successive experiments have shown that pits can be used over and over again. The positioning of pits within dwellings or under some form of shelter appears to help the storage of seed grain. Those pits that have been flooded have tended to overwhelm the excavators by the smell of fermenting grain, and have no doubt led to thoughts of beer production.

The whole range of experiments described here are part of a continuing series designed to aid our understanding of the processes of successful grain storage as well as the capabilities of prehistoric man in preserving his produce. The results can be expected to add appreciably to our knowledge of Iron Age populations in Britain.

PREPARATION AND CONSUMPTION OF FOOD

The experiments that have been carried out on the preparation of food for eating are varied, ranging from the grinding of corn and making of bread and soup, to the cutting up and cooking of meat. Some of the experiments were designed to answer specific questions relating to the function of structures, others were more general in that they tested the effect of foods on humans without any pre-conceived ideas. Between these extremes are a number of experiments where a direct approach both answered certain questions and raised new problems of further work. The first group to be described here concerns grain products, the second the preparation of meat.

Although much of the extensive literature on early cereals is based on their identification from surviving specimens, little experimental work has been done on the morphological changes that occur when grain is exposed to the conditions that eventually cause its preservation. Clearly, carbonised grain from ancient sites cannot have been in direct contact with fire, otherwise it would be consumed. Heating must have been prolonged and indirect, as under kiln conditions, and the circumstances under which carbonisation occurs on sites should be considered carefully.

Tests on the changes that take place during heating have been carried out on bread wheat (*Triticum aestivum*), barley (*Hordeum vulgare*), oats (*Avena sativa*) and rye (*Secale cereale*). Grains were measured, bottled and baked in an oven for 12 hours at 200°C. Their shrinkages were then assessed, and in general all had reduced in length, few in width, and barley had shown the least amount of change (Renfrew 1973). Such experiments seem basic to our understanding of ancient cereals by their identification on archaeological sites, particularly when new methods of recovery of such material are being successfully devised. Much work on the quantities and qualities of material recovered by various archaeological methods (e.g. Higgs 1972) must be carried out by controlled experiments before much longer; only in this way will assessments be possible of the reliability of estimated food supplies from archaeological sites, wholly dependent upon the methods of recovery adopted by the excavator (Coles 1972). This point is of course relevant not only to food remains but also to other materials (Payne 1972; Isaac 1967).

Most experimental work on the preparation of grain products has concerned their milling, and although the literature on querns and grinding stones of all types is extensive, there have been relatively few attempts to test the efficiency of such important components of domestic life. In Denmark, some minor experiments have been directed at rotary querns (Fig. 5*b*), and the results

Fig. 5

a Cooking in a skin (based on a sixteenth-century representation, Ryder, 1966)

b Grinding wheat in a quern (after Nielsen 1966)

merely confirmed widely-held beliefs that the corn acts as a lubricant in the turning of the quern, that it is less tiring to rotate the upper part completely than to move it backwards and forwards, and that a rapid turning produces a coarse flour, a slow turning yields a finer flour (Nielsen 1966).

More elaborate experiments have been carried out in Britain with similar Romano-British querns (Moritz and Jones 1950; Moritz 1958). It was found that the lower stone had to be firmly held in position, and that on a smooth surface the weight of this was not sufficient by itself. Using unroasted grain, a rotary quern produced about ·5 kg of flour at a speed of turning of 100 rev/min. It was difficult to grind a soft wheat (*Triticum vulgare*), the middlings of this tending to clog the grinding surfaces; the yield of meal extracted was low when compared with yield of a harder wheat. The best flour that could be produced would not be rated highly by modern standards. Heat-hardened grain, produced by rolling hot stones over the grain, or heating over a fire, or actually setting fire to the stalks, could be more easily ground, and it is likely that roasting of grain before grinding was practised in ancient times, as it was until recently in Scotland, Ireland and

Scandinavia. Although the materials and perhaps the methods used in this experiment could be enlarged, there are several useful observations that can be made about this work. Comparisons with size, weight and character of rotary querns in terms of their functional efficiency could easily be carried out, with particular attention to the raw materials used. The differing nature of wheat in terms of ease of grinding could also be investigated more fully, using einkorn (*T. monococcum*), emmer (*T. dicoccum*), spelt (*T. spelta*) and bread wheat (*T. aestivum*) as examples of a range of varieties; whether or not the grinding qualities of wheats affected early man's choice is debatable. Experiments have shown that even with a rotary quern, much of the grist passed through the mill unground or only partly ground. For the production of fine flour for bread, sieving and a further grinding would have been desirable, but there are few Classical references to a second grinding of wheat by Roman millers. If the grist only passed through once, sieving would have been the only method of producing flour as opposed to wholemeal for baking of bread. The question of repeated grinding, and sieving, in Roman times, is more likely to be answered by common-sense practical experiments than by interpretation of Classical literature.

A grinding experiment of a different character was that conducted on seeds of *Setaria* during the investigations in the Tehuacan Valley, Mexico (Callen 1967); the seeds were recovered from coprolites of the El Riego phase, one of the earliest periods of exploitation in the area. *Setaria* is a type of grass, the seeds of which could have been used in making bread. The plant may well have been cultivated in the area by 5000 B.C. The grains and glumes of the seeds had been crushed in a specific way, unlike those of later phases. In an experiment, *Setaria* seeds were roasted and then pounded and stirred in a mortar and pestle from the El Riego phase; the results matched those from the coprolites. Seeds crushed on a grinding stone or metate with a stone roller had a different pattern of breakage which matched the fragments from coprolites of later phases in the Tehuacan sequence, *c.* 1000 B.C. to A.D. 700.

Further experiments on mortars, saddle querns and rotary querns would be valuable. The grinding of grain in saddle querns must have been a very tiring and time-consuming job, judged by observations made among the Bemba of Zambia, where it took fully an hour to prepare the grain for one family's daily requirements (Richards 1939).

Hardening of grain before grinding could have been done in

clay ovens, such as are attested in American Indian groups and in prehistoric and historic European contexts. The manufacture of such ovens is described under the heading of pottery kilns (p. 149), but very simple ovens can be built by positioning them partly or almost wholly beneath the ground, sloping ground being of course particularly suitable. One experiment, of short duration and without rigorous recording, is nonetheless of considerable potential. The work was carried out at Lejre in Denmark, and was based upon conjectural reconstructions of Iron Age and medieval clay ovens (Nielsen 1966). Some of the house floors of these periods have traces of structures built of clay that stood within the houses; the lowest portions of the clay walls suggest that the complete structure was domed, although of uncertain height, that it measured about one metre in diameter, and that it had one small entrance at floor level. It is not known if the structure had an opening at the top, and in the experimental reconstruction, no chimney hole was provided. The experiment in fact asked one direct and leading question, did these remains represent smoke ovens? The reconstruction was based entirely upon this premise.

The oven was heated first by dry wood, which received too much air from the oven door, and was quickly consumed, producing little smoke and fierce heat. Such a form of energy could not be utilised in the attempts to reproduce a smoke oven, and was discarded. Wet or fresh wood was then used as fuel, and produced a pillar of smoke that rapidly filled the oven. The heat was sufficient to have cured meat, smoked fish, fired pots or baked food. Less wood was consumed than by an open fire, and it is likely that a turf-built or turf-roofed house would have been a safer place in which to live if it had an enclosed oven for warmth rather than an open fire; the inflammable nature of such houses has been demonstrated (p. 64).

There is no doubt that early man knew of the advantages of controlling and preserving heat; well-built hearths are known from late glacial times, *c.* 50000 B.C., and the provision of an external source of draught for an internal fireplace accords with a late glacial house, built from the bones of mammoths, in Russia. By experiment it is suggested that a canal-like passage, partly filled with charred material, at Kostienki XIX, served as a natural draught for the hearth within the house (Boriskovski 1965).

There have been relatively few attempts to experiment with the food of prehistoric man. It may be that erstwhile experimenters are too cautious to subject themselves to the possible damage or indignities caused by the consumption of exotic, ill-prepared or downright inedible foodstuffs. Or it may be that the absence of much worthwhile comparative data from ancient sites makes such experiments highly conjectural. Additionally, there is a wealth of data available from ethnographic observations about food preparation and eating habits among groups from all over the world, and this should be, and sometimes is, used as general guides to ancient practices.

Experiments dealing with the consumption of vegetable remains are few, and none of them has been as rigorous or searching as those experiments dealing with the production of food. They range from chewing bulrush to swallowing something akin to farmhouse mash, even if we exclude the highly experimental eating of a non-vegetable, the mineral mirabilite. The mineral ($Na_2SO_410H_2O$) was recovered from Salts Cave, Kentucky, and a sample was eaten to discover what would happen (Watson and Yarnell 1966); the experimenters report that 4 tablespoonfuls tasted salty and were sufficient to produce a definite laxative effect, but it is not certain if the presence of this mineral in the cave some 2500 years ago indicates such a need on the part of the original occupants.

The experiments with desert bulrush stalks (*Scirpus americanus*) were carried out on the basis of finds of quids in Danger Cave, Utah; many hundreds of these quids were found, each a small pad of matted fibres, spat out after extracting the juices by chewing (Jennings 1957). In an attempt to find out why they had been collected and taken to the site at intervals from 10000 to 4000 years ago, some stalks were chewed by the excavators in the hope that it could be determined if they had served as part of the diet, a stimulant, a narcotic, or a thirst-quencher. No narcotic or stimulant effect could be detected, and the slightly sweet taste and refreshing flavour were commented upon favourably. It was also considered that chewing might have been in part preparation of the fibres for use as rope.

A similar type of experiment was carried out in London on a replica of Tollund man's last meal. The body of Tollund man was recovered in 1950 from a peatbog in Denmark where he had lain since being strangled about 2000 years previously (Glob 1969). The conditions of preservation were such that the contents of his stomach could be examined. His last meal, eaten from 12 to 24 hours before his execution, had been entirely vegetable in origin, seeds of barley, linseed (flax), camelina (mustard), persicaria, and traces of corn spurrey, white goosefoot, wild pansy, and wild turnip seeds. There were also shreds of *Sphagnum* moss and a teaspoonful of fine sand, the former no doubt collected while drinking from a bog pool, the latter probably consumed with the ill-cleaned plant remains. None of the seeds had been roasted or baked. The linseed would have been an unlikely element to eat without soaking or boiling, as otherwise it is strongly laxative. In any case it seems probable that the plants would have been heated, into a form of soup; Classical authors record the diet of contemporary peasants as including a gruel of about 40 kg barley, 1·5 kg of linseed, 0·5 kg of coriander seeds and salt. The experimental work, if it can be called this, took place under the auspices of the BBC (Johnstone 1957). An identical assortment of seeds to those from Tollund were gathered from Kew Gardens, other botanic sources and a bird-food shop in London, and were boiled slowly with water to form an oily-looking concoction, greyish-purple in colour with orange and black flecks. This apparently did not taste as bad as it looked, and tests showed that it would have had sufficient food value to have served as a staple part of the diet. Beyond this the experiment cannot go, as there is no evidence either way to say that such a soup was a normal food for the Iron Age peoples of Denmark; the nature of Tollund man's death and burial at least suggests that the circumstances of his last meal may have been unrepresentative of the time.

These experiments with plant remains have tried to reproduce the actual food that was consumed in ancient times. A different set of experiments has also been conducted that deal entirely with the preparation and cooking of food, in this case meat. All of these have of course relied upon modern animals for their source of raw material with which to work.

Several experiments have been concerned with the cooking of meat by methods that are recorded historically or by archaeological excavation. One of these experiments was concerned with the cooking of meat in an animal skin. In theory this seemed to be adequately documented; sixteenth-century references describe and depict Irish hunting expeditions in which meat was cooked by being boiled in water in a skin suspended over a fire (Fig. 5a). '. . . after the Countrie fashion, they did cut a piece of the hide, and pricked it upon four stakes which they set about the fire, and therein they set a piece of cow for themselves . . .' (McLintock 1958, with references). A Scottish army in retreat from the English in the fourteenth century is recorded as leaving behind '. . . more than four hundred cauldrons made of hide with the hair left on, full of meat and water hung over the fire to boil . . .'.

In the event, the experimental cooking of meat in a skin was unsuccessful (Ryder 1966), and the reasons for this result were clear. The skin used was from a sheep, and was about 1·0 metre long and 0·7 metre wide; this matches the size of a fallow deer's skin, but there was about 25 mm of wool on the sheepskin and this may have caused some of the difficulties. The skin, weighing 2·2 kg, was suspended by 4 stakes (of iron as wooden stakes were not strong enough) over a fire, with the wool side down. Water was poured into the sagging skin, which held only 4·5 litres weighing 4·5 kg; even so, wooden props were needed to prevent further sagging of the skin. The depth of water in the middle was only 75 mm. The fire rapidly charred the outer wool, but great difficulty was experienced in raising the water temperature much above 50°C; the air temperature was 9°C. A lamb shank weighing ·5 kg was placed in the skin, but after several hours' stoking of the fire and replacing burnt-through wooden props, the water still had not reached above 60°C, so the meat was removed and roasted on a hot stone before consumption by a sheepdog who no doubt had enjoyed the experiment.

There was only 1 litre of water left in the skin by the end, with both leaks over the edge and evaporation combining to reduce the volume. The skin itself had shrunk by over 50 per cent and the edges were brittle, but only a small part of the wool on the outside had actually charred, the remainder having survived by water diffusing through the skin. The wool must have insulated the water from the heat. Additionally, the large area of surface water allowed surface cooling as well as evaporation. These factors must have prevented the water from heating to an appropriate degree. American Indians are recorded as using a paunch over a fire, which would have avoided the insulation problem (Driver and Massey 1957), and Ryder suggests that the Scottish haggis may have been cooked in its paunch directly over a fire. The experiment, however, had set out to reproduce the conditions as described and illustrated in ancient records, and had not been successful in achieving the predicted result.

Various authorities have recorded that it is possible to cook an animal in its own skin by sewing it up after disembowelling, then placing it in the hot embers and sands of a fire; the skin hardens and keeps the juices inside, and the meat is generally cooked, if a little rare. This is, however, a different method from cooking in a suspended skin.

A further attempt was made to boil water in an animal container by the same author (Ryder 1969). Two paunches of sheep's stomachs were suspended by strings from upright iron stakes, and 1·4 litres of water were put in each paunch. At an air temperature of 9°C, a fire beneath the paunches raised the water temperature to 60°C in one paunch, and 75°C in the other slightly lower paunch. Grain was put into one paunch to help retain heat. Hot stones were added to the other paunch and gradually the water in both increased, so that after about 3 hours, the temperatures were 90°C in the grain paunch, and 95°C in the stone paunch. In cooling, the grain helped retain the heat, and was itself cooked through. In terms of the cooking of meat, however, the small size of the paunch, and the danger that it would disintegrate if stretched out to hold meat and hot stones, suggested that the method was not entirely suitable. Yet, again, ancient references clearly state that the practicalities of cooking this way were of no great difficulty. '[The Scythians] cast all the flesh into the victims' stomachs, adding water thereto, and make a fire beneath of bones which burn finely; the stomachs easily hold the flesh when it is stripped from the bones; thus an ox serves to cook itself' (Herodotus, IV, 61). We must conclude that cooking in a skin or paunch is possible, but that it requires some experience on the part of the cook, and it is likely that there are several small tricks of the trade that are necessary to ensure success. This subject is one that could repay further experiment, as well as further study of ethnographic examples such as are described by Driver and Massey for the American Indians (1957).

It is of interest to compare this experiment with one carried out some years previously in Ireland (O'Kelly 1954). O'Kelly's work was concerned with an archaeological problem, with the reconstruction and testing of an excavated site of the sixteenth century B.C. The site, at Ballyvourney, Co. Cork, consisted of a series of post holes, stone slabs, charcoal and burnt stone heaps, and a wooden trough, all resting on or set in a peat deposit. The plan as excavated suggested that a hut or tent had stood beside an oval stone setting within which were hearths and the sunken trough (Fig. 6). The site was interpreted as a Bronze Age cooking place, by analogy with the Irish *fulacht fiadha* (deer roast).

Wooden poles were erected in the post holes, to form a tent within which stood a meat rack and a butcher's table. The wedge-shaped trough measured 1·8 × 1·0 metre, and was 0·4 metre deep; it had timber sides and the joints had been packed with peat to make it compact but not watertight. O'Kelly presumed that it had been built into the ground so that it lay beneath the natural water level and so was automatically filled with water. The trough held 450 litres of water, and beside it the two hearths were lit to heat

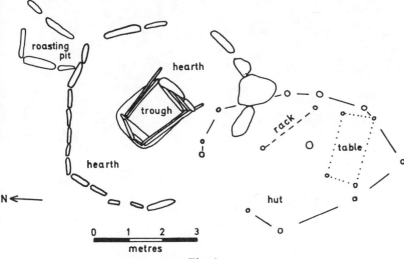

Fig. 6

Plan of cooking place at Ballyvourney, Co. Cork. Post holes mark hut and furnishings. Vertical slabs enclose hearths and roasting pit. Trough is formed of stone and wood

stones; these were dropped into the trough and within about half an hour the water began to boil. It took only a few more stones, occasionally dropped in, to keep the water near boiling temperature.

A leg of mutton weighing 5 kg was wrapped in straw, to keep it clean, and was placed in the hot water. The cooks allowed 20 minutes cooking per pound (·45 kg) and 20 minutes extra, and after 3 hours 40 minutes the mutton was extracted, perfectly clean and cooked to perfection. The sheepdogs were unrewarded as the experimenters themselves consumed the food.

Outside the oval setting where the trough lay was a stone-lined pit 2 × 1·5 metres in size, with stone slabs nearby. This was interpreted as an oven, and meat placed in it and covered by a corbelled structure of hot slabs was also well-cooked.

This experiment asked only limited but specific questions of this site. No other explanation for the site was offered, and the reconstruction to a certain extent built in its own answers. Yet the strongest support for the acceptance of this interpretation comes not only from the successful experiment but also from recorded observations of deer roasts in the same area, where comparable activities were carried out leaving comparable structures and materials behind.

Plate 1
Reconstructed Celtic chariot with Celtic ponies and driver, Hawick, Scotland; a replica made for display purposes only for a BBC School Television programme; based upon surviving cart and harness fittings from the late Iron Age in Western Europe (photo: John Coles)

Plate 2
Training cattle to pull a replica of a prehistoric ard in Denmark (from Ryder 1970)

Plate 3
Experiments with stone axes (from Stelcl and Malina 1970)
a Angle of blows with axe
b Pine tree, 40 cm diameter, after 10 minutes' work
c Pine tree felled after 21 minutes
d Spruce tree, 13 cm diameter, felled after 3 minutes

Plate 4
Reconstructed Iron Age village at Lejre, Denmark (from Ryder 1970)

Plate 5
Destruction by fire of reconstructed Iron Age house at Roskilde, Denmark (from
Nielsen 1966)

Plate 6
Experimental earthwork at Wareham, Dorset, after completion 1963 (photo: Brit. Assoc. Adv. Science, Exp. Earth. Comm.)

Plate 7
Section excavated through silting of ditch at Wareham, Dorset, after 5 years (photo: Brit. Assoc. Adv. Science, Exp. Earth. Comm.)

Plate 8
Reconstructed rampart and gateway at The Lunt, Baginton, Warwicks., from the inside (photo: Brian Hobley)

Plate 9
Ra I leaving Safi harbour in Morocco (from Heyerdahl 1971)

Plate 10
Ra I at point of abandonment. Starboard side submerged (from Heyerdahl 1971)

Plate 11
Experimental shooting of bows and arrows (from Pope 1918)
a Replica of a Turkish composite bow in reflexed position
b Replica of a Turkish composite bow, with short arrow shot through a horn;
 weight of bow 38 kg, flight of arrow 257 m
c Replica of the English long bow of yew, length 1·93 m
d Replica of the English long bow drawn to full arc, weight of bow 33 kg, flight of
 English broadhead arrow 107 m, bamboo arrow 194 m

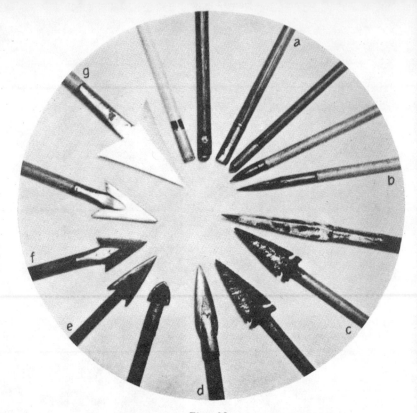

Plate 12
Arrowheads used in experimental tests (from Pope 1918)
a Blunt head tipped with 38 calibre shell *d* Metal lance used against armour
b Steel bodkin *e* Indian steel hunting head
c Obsidian arrowhead *f* Steel broadhead for killing large game
g Replica of English steel broadhead, length 89 mm, width 57 mm

Plate 13
Trepanned skull of the Early Bronze Age from Crichel Down, Dorset

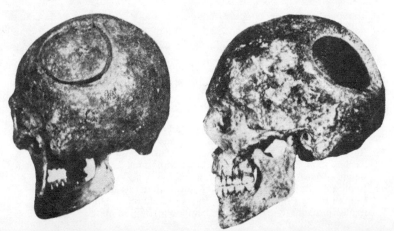

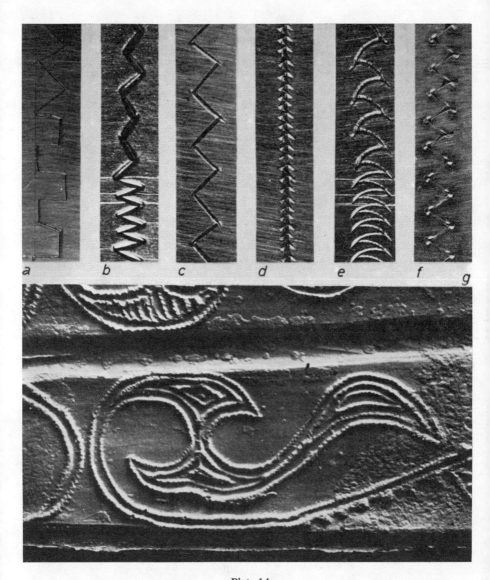

Plate 14
Experimental work on bronze with scriber (*a*), tracer (*b*), graver (*c–e*) and scorper (*f*);
g detail of mould of Iron Age scabbard plate from Lisnacrogher, Ireland, to show
tool marks (photo: R. L. Wilkins)

Plate 15
Reconstructed Roman ballista (photo: L. P. Morley)

Plate 16
Testing of metal shield (*left*) and leather shield with Bronze Age swords (photo:
Ralph Crane *Life* © 1963 *Time Inc.*)

Plate 17
Reconstructed Romano-British kiln at Barton-on-Humber, Lincs., ready for firing.
Piled bricks for blocking flue and vent. Kiln load ready for insertion in background
(photo: H. Atkinson)

Plate 18
Painting of an eland from Bellevue, Cape Province, South Africa; the body is in
red-brown, the neck, head and inner-legs are in white (length of animal 37 cm)

2

HEAVY INDUSTRY

HOUSE-BUILDING AND DESTRUCTION

Although experiments dealing with ancient agriculture have interested archaeologists for many years, it is only relatively recently that attention has also been directed to another important aspect of early communities, the provision for shelter in houses and behind earth and stone ramparts. There have been a number of such experiments, and several of these are of particular importance. In Denmark, a group of Iron Age houses has been built at Lejre (Pl. 4), to help contain some of the experimental work carried out at the Historisk-Arkaeologisk Forsogscenter (p. 169).

In 1956–8, Hansen undertook the reconstruction of Neolithic houses of the third millennium B.C. at Allerslev, Zealand, Denmark (Fig. 7a). The plans adopted were of rectangular and apsidal houses, based on excavations at Troldebjerg (Hansen 1961, 1962). The houses were of wattle and daub construction, with thatched roofs.

The posts that provided the firm support for the walls and roof were set in post holes dug into the ground or in a foundation trench with stone packing for the posts. The walls were made of osier wattling which held clay thrown and smoothed on both inner and outer faces. The quantity of material required to build the long rectangular house, which measured 15 × 6 metres in plan, was remarkably large. Nine tonnes of clay, mixed with hay and water and kneaded by bare feet and hands, and 2000 osiers and hazel branches were used for the walls, as well as timber supports. The wooden posts needed for uprights, beams and

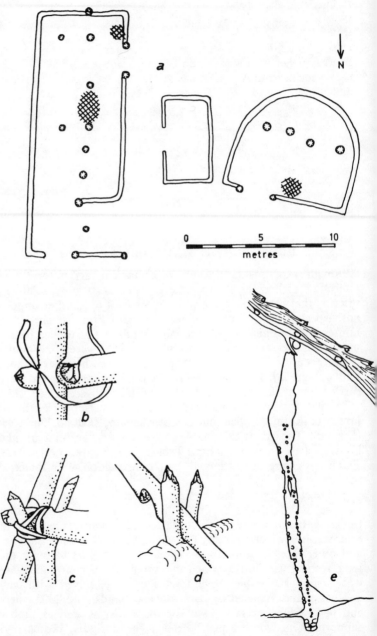

Fig. 7

rafters totalled 6 dozen, the rafter poles 4 metres long, the other poles up to 2·5 metres long. One hundred laths and other rods were also needed for the roof, which was made of 220 bundles of reeds and rushes; elm-bark strips were used to tie beams and posts together (Fig. 7b–d), and neither wood nails nor any other nails were needed. A load of hay and masses of stones for the floor and hearth completed the materials for this small house.

Little difficulty was experienced in the building operations, but it required about 12 men working for 10 days actually to put the house up after collecting the materials. Estimates were made of this part of the exercise, on the basis of some experimental work and modern observations; allowing for a 10-hour working day, it would take 4 man-days to prepare the posts and poles, 10 man-days to cut the hay and reeds, 8 man-days to cut the osiers and laths, 5 man-days to dig the clay, and about 5 man-days to transport it all to the site. The grand total of effort required to collect and transport the materials, and then to build the house, was estimated at 150 man-days, and so could have been accomplished by a small party of men, or men and women, numbering about a dozen and working for 2 weeks. This is still a sizeable work party, and another estimate might be a family group of 4 or 5 able-bodied members working for 5 weeks, supporting themselves in terms of food and shelter meantime.

On the basis of observations made in upper Canada in the late eighteenth and nineteenth centuries, there is no doubt that a log-cabin type of shelter is far more easily constructed than one of wattle and daub (Guillet 1963). A log-cabin, 6 × 4 metres in plan, requiring no foundation trench and a minimum of materials other than tree stems of uniform diameter, but not necessarily wedge-split, could be erected from scratch in 4 man-days. If stone axes in place of steel axes were used, this might increase the time required to fell and fashion the timber by a small amount (p. 20), but in no way could the total approach the 150 man-days required

Fig. 7

a   Schematic plan of houses at Allerslev, Denmark, showing foundation trenches, post holes (circles) and hearths (hatched)

b–d   Joins of timbers: b, simple join held by elm bark lacing; c, tie between post, tie beam (horizontal) and rafter; d, rafter riding into fork of post at top of wall

e   Section through eroded wall. Wattle walling shown by small circles, major crack in clay at middle of wall, and cone of washed mud from wall on outside. Height of wall 2 m

(after Hansen 1961)

for the admittedly more elaborate, larger and more wind-proof wattle and daub house.

This recorded ease in building with logs may help to explain the popularity of such structures within some of the impressively large burial mounds in Europe. Estimates of the amount of time required in piling up these mounds (p. 73), without log-built structures within them, could be reduced dramatically by the incorporation of these prefabricated wooden structures, allowing a result of impressive appearance for minimum effort.

Another Neolithic house was built at Lough Gur in Co. Limerick, Ireland, based upon the plans of houses excavated there by Ó Ríordáin, 1939–55. The work was financed by the BBC for a television programme, and this is only one of a number of experimental archaeological studies that have interested television authorities both in Britain and abroad. The plan of the original Lough Gur houses had been represented by post holes and stone settings, and the reconstruction was based so far as was possible on the archaeological evidence (Johnstone 1957). The house was oblong, 10 × 6 metres, and was built on a slope. Most of the materials used in the reconstruction were produced by modern methods, although some of the ropes used for tying the rafters and roof beams to the upright posts were made of twisted rushes (sugans); these were produced by twirling rushes round a stick that was then twirled as more rushes were added to the end of the growing rope, in comparable fashion to Heyerdahl's papyrus boat (p. 109).

The problem with all such reconstructions is that we lack adequate evidence about wall heights and roofing materials; the character of the walls themselves can sometimes be recovered by surviving parts of wattle and daub construction, but if clay does not survive or is not recognised, then the tendency must be to fall back upon turf, wood or reed walls. Turf or thatch for roofing would also be difficult to distinguish from surviving pieces. And a log-cabin type of house, with little foundation work required, would leave virtually no trace at all in the ground for archaeologists to recognise except perhaps the short stakes driven in at intervals to prevent log slip.

In Britain, many remains of Iron Age round houses have been recovered through increasingly expert excavation. Some of these remains consist of an almost-circular gully within which may appear stake holes at intervals with stone and earth packing material adjacent. Larger stake or post holes sometimes occur at the ends of the gully, and mark doorway positions. There is a great variety in the plans of these structures, and a generalised plan was used for the experimental reconstruction of one of these stake-built houses (Reynolds 1972). The plan for this was based upon recent excavations at Breiddin, Montgomeryshire, and South Cadbury, Somerset, and the house was erected at the Avoncroft Museum of Buildings, near Bromsgrove, Worcestershire.

A circular gully was dug, 30 cm wide and 15 cm deep, with a diameter of 7·5 metres. Sharpened stakes, 1·8 metres long, were driven vertically into the gully from 30 to 60 cm apart, packed with earth and stones, and withies were woven in and out to form basket-like walls ready for clay daub. The stake tops were notched to carry a ring-beam of withies lashed together with leather thongs on both sides of the stakes. Six roof poles were then raised, notched and tied at both apex and ring-beam to form the framework for the roofing which could have been of thatch. The only problem was the precise attachment of the roof poles to the ring-beam; by notching the poles twice, they fitted onto the ring-beam withies on both sides of the vertical wall-stakes, so that the weight of the roof was spread downwards onto the stakes and not left pushing entirely outwards on the outer part of the ring-beam. The upper ends of the roof poles were held apart by the use of another ring-beam, to avoid choking the apex of the house with timber. Estimates of the time required for the preparation of materials and erection of the house were not completed, but it is likely to have been comparable to that of the Danish rectangular house.

The conjectured form of the circular house differs in little degree from recent round houses built by shepherds in central Italy. One of these, observed in 1964, was 5 metres in diameter, and was built almost entirely of wood, straws and reeds (Close-Brooks and Gibson 1966). The details appear in Fig. 8; the roof poles are tied with wire to the wall posts but several of the rafters are longer and extend through the wall to form a buttress. A ring-beam of withies is woven around the junction of posts and rafters to prevent the wall posts being pushed outwards by the roof weight. The roof of thatch is reinforced by horizontal beams 3·25 metres above the floor. The walls are of straw and reed held by withies and lashed onto the wall posts. The door post pivots in a horizontal log, the top of the post held loosely in a forked branch. This small house slept 6, in bunks, and there was room for a hearth with suspended pot, and racks for holding slaughtered lambs.

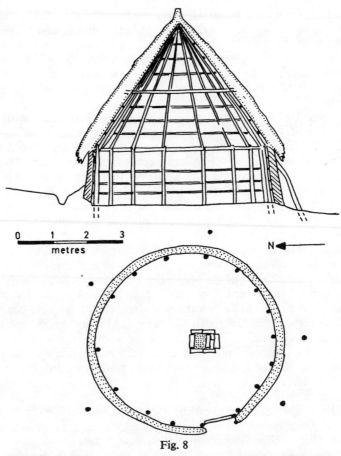

Fig. 8

Internal view and ground plan of round hut near Rome (after Close-Brooks and Gibson 1966)

Apart from the variable internal structures, which would in this case leave traces of post holes (bunk supports) and hearth, the only surviving elements of this stake house after decay would be the circular ring of post holes. The reconstruction of such post holes into a functional dwelling could be entirely conjectural, it could be based upon actual rebuilding, or it might be understood through observation of recent examples. The combination of the last two lines of reasoning help support the first.

Similar types of house, built of wooden poles or posts in narrow foundation trenches, have been reconstructed in Tennessee on the basis of excavated plans (Nash 1968). A series of mounds along the banks of the Duck River consisted of collapsed houses with remains of charred poles, grass from thatched roofs, burnt clay from walls, and multiple post or pole holes. The houses were occupied from about A.D. 1000–1600.

The earlier type of house is described as 'small pole' form because, when rebuilt, it had slender poles set closely together in a trench or gully and packed with stone, earth or logs. The poles stretched vertically upwards and were then bent over and interwoven to form a roof, their other ends set in the opposing gully of the roughly square house plan; the effect is of course that of an upside-down giant basket. Horizontal laths were tied onto these uprights, and clay was plastered to form air-tight walls, with straw thatching above.

The later type of house in the area, the 'large log' form, was also rebuilt. The logs were set in post holes, not in a gully, and stood under 2 metres high; horizontal logs were attached to the tops of these uprights, and supported the roof rafters which converged to a peak. Horizontal panelling, clay, plaster, and thatching completed this house, and the point was made that in external appearance both 'small pole' and 'large log' houses looked the same; the absence of much archaeological evidence about roofing forms and materials must allow some uncertainty about final versions, and thick thatch may disguise a multitude of differences in the functional efficiency of varying roof supports.

The 'small pole' form of house is broadly similar to a British Iron Age house built on Bredon Hill in 1966 (Reynolds 1967). The aims of this experiment were to calculate the speed of building and the constructional details of the roof. The plan was based upon excavated houses at the Glastonbury lakeside village, where the only evidence for roofing was collapsed and preserved thatch and central supporting posts. 41 ash poles, 2–4m long, were used, 19 of these as upright wall posts, 19 as roofing poles and 3 as a central tripod for the roof. Withies were woven around the wall posts, and a plaster of clay, chopped straw and water was applied to the walls. Withies were loosely woven around the roof poles to support sheaves of straw for the thatched roof. After 9 months the hut was burned down by vandals, but the archaeologists could observe that the collapsed straw roof left 30cm of ash on the floor of the hut, that the fallen roof poles left charcoal lines across the floor, and that the inner clay wall was partly fired hard. The time taken to build this hut, 4m in diameter, was about 175 man-hours, plus the additional time needed to obtain materials.

The roof proved very simple to devise and construct, and no problems over lateral pressure on the walls from the weight of the roof were experienced.

Collaboration between specialists in such small house-building operations would without question eliminate much duplication of effort as well as allow the pooling of information; the numerous reconstructions of small buildings in Austria, from late glacial tents to Iron Age log houses, provide a good range of the possibilities (Hampl 1968).

Another problem of Iron Age archaeology is that concerning the interpretation of simple rectangular post hole settings within Iron Age settlements and hill-forts. Such settings sometimes occur away from the houses, and they have been interpreted as grain storehouses, fighting and observation platforms, or barns for hay. The first of these is perhaps less likely now that experiments have shown how easy it is to store grain underground. The second explanation is based upon ethnographic evidence from New Zealand, and is certainly attractive for some hill-forts in southern Britain. The third, a bit more prosaic, has been tested by experiment (Reynolds 1972).

The reconstruction was based upon a plan of post settings from the Iron Age farmstead of Tollard Royal, Wiltshire. The four post holes were used to hold vertical posts supporting a slightly raised wooden floor, a framework for a sloping turf roof, and supporting cross-beams. The structure had wattle walling in part, and a shed of $2 \cdot 4 \times 1 \cdot 8$ metre floor area would hold the straw from about $\cdot 1$ hectare, enough to thatch the roof of a small round house. This experimental reconstruction demonstrated that a barn could be built using only 4 post holes as archaeological evidence; the explanation, however, of 4 post hole settings on prehistoric sites still is subject to conjecture, and it may well be that some held barns, but others held platforms for observation or drying food or exposing the dead.

These reconstructions are but one aspect of the way in which experimental archaeology can help our understanding of prehistoric houses. Simple replications can provide a range of the possible ways by which ancient man constructed shelters for himself, and so long as the rebuilt structures do not wilfully diverge from the archaeological record these can be no cause for uncertainty. Where the problems arise, however, are in the upper parts of houses, roofing in particular, and it is here that much experimental work could be done on types of roof, quantities of materials and procedures, and the efficiency of roofs in retaining heat but not smoke, in providing air but not water for the occupants.

Archaeological problems of excavation can also be approached through the replication of houses followed by their planned use or destruction. A sequence of excavation plan→reconstruction→ destruction→excavation plan provides a model which can be tested for fit. Such work has only been adequately done in Denmark.

The Neolithic houses built at Allerslev in 1956–8 were observed over several years, particularly about the processes of decay that became active as soon as the house was built. The drying of the clay walls produced some cracking, and rain eroded parts of the walls, but rising damp was the greatest danger to the structure. The thickness of the wall bases was much reduced by damp and this was apparent on both inner and outer faces; frost was a major agency on both faces (Fig. 7e). A stone base would have prevented such heavy damage which extended as much as ·5 metre up the walls. The eroded matter from the walls piled up against the base. All of this damage occurred within 3 or 4 years of the building of the houses.

The small rectangular house (Fig. 7a) was occupied for a time to see how it suited modern living processes; this was not a valid exercise in terms of reproducing the deposits of occupation likely to have been formed by prehistoric man. Modern habits and customs, the whole approach to existence, are likely to be different from those of early man, but the main problem is that the differences cannot be measured. We really can have little idea about the cleanliness, tidiness, domestic mobility and population that combined with other factors, food supplies, sleeping habits and the like, to make up the sparse or plentiful 'occupation' debris that was accumulated in and around ancient dwellings. Ethnographic observations are not likely to be useful in this connection. In the experimental occupation of this house, potsherds were scattered around the floor and there was a hearth that contributed ash to the other debris which gradually appeared, including soil tramped in from outside.

The smoke from the fire tended to circulate around the upper interior of the house before drifting through a hole in the roof or filtering through the roof itself. The smoke was dense at times, hanging in the air, so that the only relatively clear air available to the occupants extended from the floor upwards to a height of 1·5 metres. The inhabitants presumably spent much time lying down or sitting up, not standing. Another recorded feature of the fire was that it tended to blacken the upper part of the walls and the roof, so that it might appear to an excavator, searching in the rubble of a collapsed and decayed house, that the building had been destroyed by fire; this is an interesting point well worth further examination and experiment. In the event, the hearth was used once too often, and in 1958 sparks caught on the dried partly charred roof and the house burnt down.

The opportunity was not missed to excavate the remains. Only the osiers remained upright, and the clay of the walls had been baked to a depth of 5 mm on the inside, and almost totally through at the top. Much of this clay soon flaked away, and pieces were recovered that matched the mud plaster from the original house at Troldebjerg. The roof posts and beams had turned into thin ash lines where they had fallen; the posts in particular had stood firm until the blazing roof fell in and ignited them at the base.

This experiment in testing the replicated structures through occupation and destruction showed the value of both aspects of experimental archaeology, as well as the limitations in the amount of information, out of the vast bulk of potential data, that could be of use in archaeological explanations. It also showed the spectacular nature of a burning thatched house, and in 1962 the Danish television authorities undertook the reconstruction of a long house and its destruction by fire (Nielsen 1966).

The model adopted was that of an Iron Age house excavated in 1937 (Fig. 9). The plan showed a foundation trench measuring 14 × 6 metres with slightly rounded corners. Stake holes in the trench showed that the house had been of wattle and daub construction. Within the house were large post holes for roof supports, post holes on one side of the central doors for partitions or stalls for cattle, and a packed clay floor on the other side which with a central hearth must have been the living quarters (Hansen 1966).

The reconstructed house was duly erected with considerable care (Fig. 10). The outer lower walling was buttressed by turf and stone to hold the very heavy thrust of the roofing timbers and its weighted thatch. All the timbers in the house were marked with sheet metal numbers, and thermocouples were placed at various positions to record the temperature of the conflagration. Domestic objects, pottery, baskets and boxes, and general stores, were placed around to simulate possible ancient materials. Brush wood was then piled against the side of the house and set alight in a stiff breeze. The results were spectacular and swift, both admirably suited for TV; the fire swept into the house and rapidly burnt

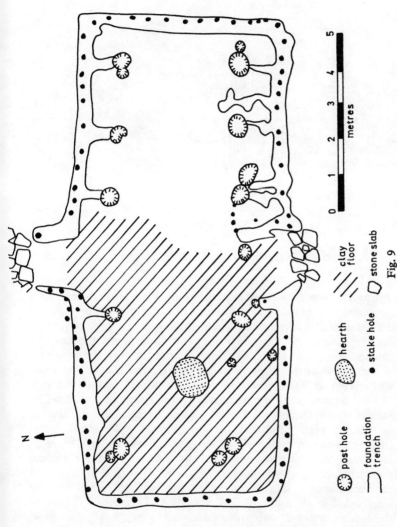

N

metres

Fig. 9

Plan of Iron Age house as excavated, the basis for the reconstruction in Fig. 10 (after Hansen 1966)

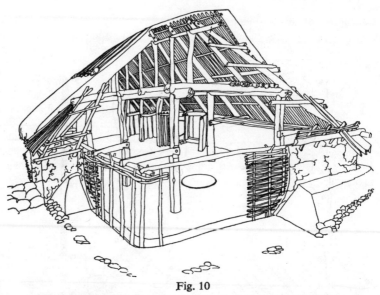

Fig. 10

Reconstructed Iron Age house near Roskilde, Denmark (after Hansen 1966)

through the top of the roof (Pl. 5). Within a few minutes the entire structure was burning fiercely, and in 20 minutes the structure collapsed. After 35 minutes it had disintegrated completely, leaving only the heavy upright posts protruding above the heap of charred wood and ashes. The temperature through the long axis of the house at floor level reached 900°C, and that at the walls was just under 700°C, sufficient to bake some of the mud walling.

After 6 months the site was excavated so that material could be located and inspected, the metal tags of timbers plotted, and an excavation plan produced for comparison with the original (Fig. 11). The correlation of plans was quite remarkable. Of greater advantage was the realisation that specific objects—door frames, partitions, flooring—could be recognised, if with difficulty, and that ephemeral traces elsewhere on ancient sites might well be interpreted in the light of this new data. This surely is one of the achievements of experimental archaeology, that it can yield not only answers to questions asked but answers to questions unasked.

One or two other structures have also been subjected to destruction by fire, but they have not yielded the data that was obtained from the Danish work. The use of scale models for such

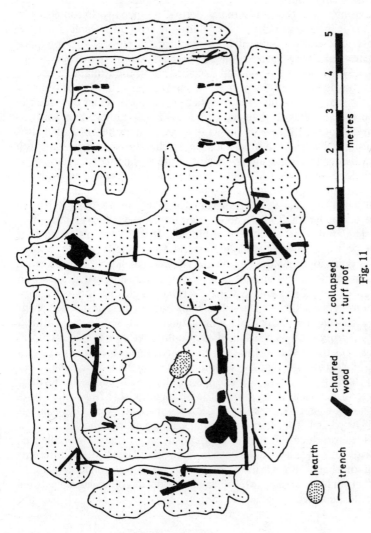

hearth

trench

charred
wood

collapsed
turf roof

metres

0 1 2 3 4 5

Fig. 11

General plan of excavated replica Iron Age house after destruction by fire (after Hansen 1966)

testing provides an easy source of information but its relevance is doubtful (Smith 1953).

Experimental firing of turf, thatch and timber houses has demonstrated that incendiary action is speedily executed, and there is little or no chance of saving the structure. Such is not the case with houses built of mud brick or rubble walls. No experiments have been carried out on these structures but observations made during some organised destruction on the Indian–Afghanistan border in 1919–20 may be of interest (Gordon 1953). During some troubles in this area, it was apparently necessary to destroy the native villages. The huts in the villages had rubble walls, a single door with few or no windows, and a solid roof of beams with brushwood and mud packing. In this situation a casual torch applied to the building would not ignite it. The technique devised for this necessary task was to break holes in the roof and walls for an air supply, to stack masses of brushwood inside the house, to blow up the roof supports with explosive, and to pour kerosene onto the wood. Once these preliminaries were over, the huts were demolished with little difficulty. It was also observed that the occupants were not likely to stand aside quietly while the work was going on, and the engineers required considerable protection from the irate natives. This is why the technique of destruction was called 'Fire and Sword'. Archaeologically the operation demonstrated the resistance of such huts to fire, and it was concluded that far more huts would have collapsed from rain and weathering than as a result of accidental, perhaps even deliberate, fire. Yet the fact that the internal hearth produced much ash and smoke during normal use would ensure that such huts, when they had collapsed through erosion, would contain debris that might suggest destruction by fire to the archaeologist. Mud-walled huts of south-eastern Europe have been observed to have a life-span of 15–20 years before they are virtually unrepairable and, as a rough guide, produce ·3 metre of deposit when they do collapse; conditions in the Middle East may not have been much different. All of these observations are of relevance to archaeology, and experimental excavation of such modern collapsed structures would be useful.

EARTHWORKS AND EROSION

A second major field of enquiry into the construction and decay of ancient monuments concerns earthworks of various types. These may be of loose stone, soil or turf, with or without timber-lacing, and although experiments in the building of these, and in recording their decay, have been few, the results have been important. More work has been done upon the erosion of the ditches that generally provided the raw materials for the earthworks, but here there is much room for further work on a variety of soils.

One of the first archaeologists to attempt to understand the processes of erosion of ditches and banks was Pitt-Rivers. In 1893, during his total excavation of the Wor Barrow in Cranborne Chase, Dorset, he emptied the ditches surrounding the barrow and left them exposed to rain and frost (Pitt-Rivers 1898). His aim was to discover by experiment the rate of silting of the ditches and thereby the time that had elapsed since they had been excavated as sources of material for the long barrow. After 4 years, he excavated sections through the accumulated silt which had already reached depths of 70cm. He observed that the top of the ditch had weathered by almost 50cm and that the silt contained lenses of dark earth from fallen turf; the shape of the ditch had altered because the rapid silting had protected the base from weathering, while expanding the width at the top. He was not able to gain an idea of the elapsed time since the ditches had originally been dug in Neolithic times because the initial silting was so rapid, and the subsequent silting therefore so slow.

Comparable observations were made by Curwen in 1929 on the weathering of military trenches dug in Sussex in 1915–16 (Curwen 1930b). These showed that the ditch sides had originally been much steeper, that silting was rapid in the first years, and that the banks thrown up in front of the trenches tended to settle outwards, increasing their width appreciably and not reducing their height by much. Atkinson's work at Dorchester, Oxford, showed that 75cm of gravel silt accumulated in a ditch of a small henge monument in only 3 months (Atkinson *et al.* 1951).

These observations emphasised the need for a detailed experiment on silting processes extended over a long period, and they led onto the organisation of effort that resulted in the building of the experimental earthwork at Overton Down near Marlborough in Wiltshire, which represents the most ambitious attempt yet to understand the processes of erosion and weathering of ancient monuments (Jewell 1963).

The Overton Down earthwork was constructed in 1960 through the work of a committee of the British Association for the Advancement of Science, in collaboration with many specialists and interested parties. The site selected was on chalk, an obvious choice in view of the great quantity of impressive prehistoric monuments in the chalk of southern England. Various principles were laid down relating to the need for accuracy in building the earthwork and digging the ditch so that future excavations could be related to the original form. The bank and ditch were to approximate in profile to prehistoric monuments, the ditch with steeply-sloped sides and flat bottom; the bank was to have a core of turf and topsoil, and within the bank was to be buried a range of samples (Fig. 12). Other samples were to be scattered around the site before work began, to see how they fared. Finally, part of the work was to be done with primitive tools.

The bank as constructed was nearly 21 m along the crest, at a uniform height of 2 m, and a width at base of 7 m; it had a turf core covered by topsoil, with 3 layers of chalk rubble on top. The angle of each layer was 30° from the horizontal, which was 5° less than the angle of rest for piled chalk rubble. Between one edge of the bank and the quarry ditch was a berm of unaltered ground, 1·3 m wide. The ditch was 3 m wide at the top and 2·4 m at the bottom, and was dug 1·5 m into the chalk (cf. Pl. 6).

A number of enamelled steel tubes were erected first along the central line of the proposed bank. The turf from the ditch area was cut and stacked in four dwindling rows (Layer A). Polythene tubes were placed vertically at the sides of the stack, and numbered pottery discs were put on the turf stack. A second layer (B), of topsoil from the ditch area, was dumped over the stack, and pottery was placed on both sides of this bank.

The ditch was then excavated from the solid chalk and tipped onto the bank to form three more layers (C, D, E). A template was provided to ensure that the quarry ditch was of uniform size throughout its length, and strings controlled the dumping onto the bank so that it too was of a standard shape. Layer C was the first to be put down, and consisted of the uppermost chalk which was weathered more than the lower chalk for Layers D and E. Road-stone chips were scattered over C to separate it from D, and a second row of polythene tubes was erected along the edge of C. Various materials (see below) were placed on top of C, and flints were put onto the turf beside C to be covered by the chalk of D.

Layer D was of cleaner, harder chalk from the ditch, and covered C. Roadstone chips and pottery discs were put onto the top of the bank, and discs were also placed on the turf beside D, to be covered by E. The chalk for E was then extracted from the ditch, now nearly in its final shape, and tipped onto the bank. The ditch sides were then cut back to the required angle, and the ditch floor made level. The material from the ditch sides was put on top of

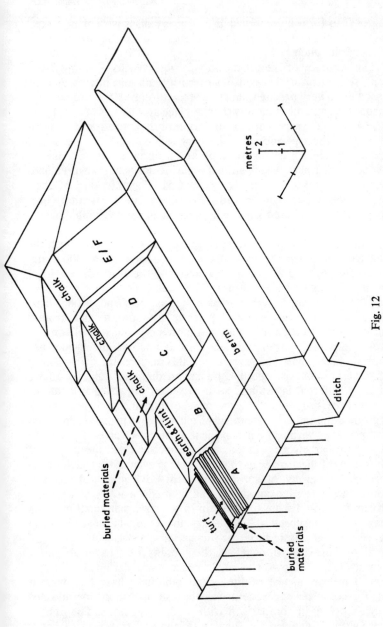

Fig. 12

Overton Down earthwork, isometric drawing showing consecutive layers (after Jewell 1963)

Layer E to form a combined E/F. Pottery discs were then placed on top of the bank, on its lower slope, and on the turf on both sides of the ditch.

The accuracy of the operation was observed to be about 1 per cent, so that future excavations of both bank and ditch would be based upon very precise data. The excavation of 1·5 metre sections through bank and ditch was to take place at intervals of 2, 4, 8, 16, 32, 64 and 128 years, with examination of the ditch after 3 months and other short periods.

The materials buried within, on and around the bank consisted of textiles, leathers, wood, animal bone including human, cremated human bone, flints, and clay potsherds. The intention of their burial was to determine, through subsequent excavation, how they had been altered physically and chemically through burial, weathering and decay.

The Overton Down earthwork was duplicated in 1963 with the construction of another experimental bank and ditch at Wareham, Dorset (Pl. 6). The subsoil here is sand, and the heathland environment contains heather and pine. The bank consists of a turf stack and layers of sand, with buried materials of wood, stone, fired clay, bone, textiles, hide and glass, placed on the old ground surface beneath the turf stack, and between two layers of sand.

A comparable experiment, but on a much smaller scale, has recently been devised (Ascher 1970); this involves the construction of circular mounds, about 2 metres in diameter and 0·5 metre high, of different layers and with materials buried to test rate of decay. Provision for excavation of segments, and accurate recording of slumping and movement of materials, is provided by posts and poles set within the mound just as in the Overton Down and Wareham earthworks. The advantage of the small mounds is of course that they are cheap to construct, and by testing such structures on a variety of soils in different environmental settings, comparative results could be readily made available. The disadvantage would seem to be again in the size, that small mounds may well not represent adequately the compaction and decay processes that obtain in larger life-size earthworks.

All of these operations reflect the subsequent excavation plans, and at Overton Down the whole process was designed with this aim. The only aspect of the actual building phase that was in itself a complete experiment was the use of ancient methods of earth-moving, in comparison with modern methods. The first of these studies involved the digging, lifting and transport of chalk with modern steel picks, shovels and buckets. No wheelbarrows were used. The weight of ·028 cubic metre (1 cubic foot) of solid moist chalk was almost exactly 50 kg. By timed runs, a working day rate of 750 kg per man-hour was estimated as reasonable for a determined worker using modern tools. This could then be compared with the rate for a man using ancient tools.

The tools selected for the second study were shed red deer antlers, ox and horse scapulae, and wicker baskets. The antlers had the bez- and trez-tines cut off. In use they served well as picks, actually being swung freely into the chalk; they were also used as wedges with oak mauls, and as levers. In all these tasks they were extremely useful implements, and did not break or show many signs of wear.

The scapulae were employed as shovels, and although the horse scapulae were favoured, neither was very efficient in lifting chalk; they were too narrow. When used as a scraper, however, they served well to pull the chalk rubble into the baskets. It is likely that wooden shovels of almost any reasonable shape would have been more efficient than the scapulae. One modern shoveller could both fill and carry buckets for a pickman, but with the scapulae and baskets it took two workers to keep up with a pickman using antler, and the difference was solely due to the shovel difference.

In timed runs, it was found that a work rate using the ancient implements was 250 kg per man-hour, with an average basket load of 13·5 kg. The ratio for modern: ancient tools was therefore 3:1 over short-timed runs, but another and perhaps fairer comparison, based on recorded overall rates throughout the work, was only 1·3:1·0; in either case the difference was due to the superiority of the shovel over the scapula.

The total time spent on the work of digging the ditch and building the bank, with 4 full-time supervisors, was 1543 man-hours, the supervisors contributing 388 to this total. In terms of total time, however, allowance would have to be made for the sheltering and feeding of the workers. The volume of the whole ditch excavated was 113·75 cubic metres, and therefore estimates could be made of the time necessary for the actual digging and transporting of chalk for prehistoric monuments. These are notoriously subject to uncertainties, but one estimate for the building of an average-sized round barrow, 12 metres in diameter, might be 6–8 workers for 2 weeks. Such conjectures are useful because the figures are small and such barrows are one-period structures. Much less reliable are figures for the construction of enormous monuments, Silbury Hill or Avebury for example, the former involving perhaps 50 million basketfuls of earth, the latter requiring perhaps 1·5 million man-hours. The quantity of people required for these, and therefore the time, is almost totally inestimable.

A recent observation of bank-building in Nigeria is distinctly relevant here (Shaw 1970). The objective was to raise an earthen embankment about 50 metres long, fully 4 metres high, and wide enough to carry a roadway along the top. The volume could be estimated as 800 cubic metres, and the bank was raised in less than a day by a large number of men without lifting any earth at all. The tool used was a short-handled hoe, and the workers used this both as a pick for loosening the earth and as a scraper for dragging the earth towards themselves and between their legs to another worker behind. In this way, with rows of 8 to 10 men, the earth was dragged over the ground and gradually up to form the bank. Of course there was no steep-sided ditch to dig, but the prehistoric scapula, so inefficient as a lifting tool, would have served well as a scraper in this particular way. The Nigerian observations are useful in indicating that there are other ways to build banks and move earth than by carrying material.

Some experiments have been carried out with ancient types of digging and carrying implements. The unsuitability of the ox scapula as a shovel was commented upon by Curwen (1926) as a result of comparative work on chalk rubble; it was found that lifting with a scapula took four times as long as with a pointed army spade, and slightly more time than bare hands.

During his excavations in the flint mines of Cissbury, Sussex, General Pitt-Rivers experimented with antler tools, making picks, wedges and punches from a pair of antlers. Two men, one of them the general himself, then dug out a cubic yard (*c.* 1 cubic metre) in 1·5 hours; the flint mine under excavation had a gallery about 9 metres long, and this then might have been dug out in 12 hours. The wedges, driven in with a punch, served to detach nodules of flint from the chalk. Ox scapula shovels were used to fill a wheelbarrow in slightly more time than with the bare hands, and the general commented that although the scapula was less efficient, the saving to the hands might have been important.

A similar type of exercise was mounted during the examination of Maya *chultuns* or storage pits in Guatemala (Puleston 1971). In experiments dealing with food storage (p. 41), a *chultun* was dug in the limestone bedrock, using bifacially-worked flints hafted with wooden handles. The flints were adequate for cutting through the upper hard limestone and for digging out part of the softer material below, but narrow portions of the *chultun* required a long-handled bit-like tool, devised on the spot. It took only 30 man-hours to complete the *chultun* with the aid of a basketeer.

All of these experimental excavations have shown fairly consistent work rates for digging and transporting material, principally chalk, and as such, the body of opinion thus expressed may be taken as an accurate estimate of the work potential of ancient man. This can be of considerable value in considering the labour necessary for earthwork raising, but probably only for small monuments where the physical size of the structure suggests a small group of labourers. Round barrows are a good example of this, but long barrows could also be considered along these lines. Judged from the experimental work carried out on chalk and on other materials, there seems some reason to suppose that excavations of ancient structures of these types might well be designed to look for the separation of work parties on the basis of different work rates and areas on a particular site. This would possibly be the only way by which the other factor in building operations, that of the size of the working party and therefore the time, could be assessed. It is really of little value to conjecture that a monument could have been built by one man in 1000 days or 1000 men in one day, or any permutation between.

The Overton Down earthwork is probably the best source of ancient work rates and the volume by basketfuls of a chalk-built structure. Its second and main purpose, however, was not this but was to allow excavation and observation of the erosion, weathering and decay of the bank and ditch over a period of decades (Jewell and Dimbleby 1968).

A small area of the ditch was sectioned in early 1961, 7½ months after it had been excavated out of the chalk. This was to discover the nature of the scree that had fallen into the ditch. The silt had covered the angles of the bottom and side walls up to 30 cm above the ditch floor. It rested at a silt angle of 36°, and at Overton Down this did not reach to the centre of the ditch floor which remained clear. After 20½ months, it was observed that the scree reached almost one metre in thickness at the ditch sides while, above, the ditch walls had collapsed so that the turf was deeply undercut and drooping. After 25½ months, the first undercut turf fell and rolled to the centre of the ditch floor, where the first silting had just occurred. The scree was of alternating fine and coarse chalk rubble, representing summer and winter deposition. A notable observation, confirming Pitt-Rivers and Curwen, was that the angle of the ditch sides was preserved at the base of the sides where the first silt had come to rest; this is a point well worth emphasis. After 32 months the scree was 1·25 metres deep, and the undercut turf had fallen into the ditch. After 48 months the scree had slumped by rainfall, the fallen turf had sprouted if it landed upright, the other turf was disintegrating, and the chalk silt had achieved an angle of repose of 32°. The other main point worth emphasis was that the silt at the bottom of the centre of the ditch need not have been contemporary with the ditch; objects, for instance Mesolithic flints, that had lain in the old turf for centuries before the ditch was cut could have fallen onto the ditch bottom, at its centre, through the erosion of the uppermost chalk and the fall of the turf. Such finds at the base of the ditch are clearly not contemporary with the ditch and should not be used to date it.

At the same time as the ditch fill was being examined, sections into the bank were cut, at 7½, 20½, 25½, 32 and 48 months. Some slumping of the deposits was recorded, mainly due to the compression of Layers A and B, and the bank began to spread sideways. The buried materials began to show signs of decay; in the chalk, the linen textiles were the best preserved, but most were disintegrated in the turf layer. Leathers had not altered much, and changes in the bones were slight (Garlick 1969). *Lycopodium* spores dusted to simulate pollen rain in 1960 during the construction of the earthwork had moved both up and down through earthworm activity. Moles had invaded the bank and thrown out some of the roadstone chips from the Layer C/D interface. A potsherd had moved from the original land surface beneath the bank to the tailing of the final Layer E/F.

At Wareham in Dorset, sections have been excavated through the bank and ditch silting after one year and subsequently (Fig. 13 and Pl. 7). The results are not yet published, but several important aspects have already become clear. After nine years, vegetation including pine trees was growing on the edge of the bank, partly on the surface of slumped washed material, and this growth was effectively preventing sand from filtering down into the ditch; the effects of this development are of interest for the excavation and interpretation of areas between original banks, barrows and ramparts on the one hand, and their ditches on the other, where interaction of bank spread, ditch edge collapse, and vegetation, including deep-rooted plants, may well be complex and greatly dependent on particular soils.

It has been said that the recording of erosion and weathering in these banks and ditches is of limited value because it is erosion and decay over centuries and millennia that archaeologists en-

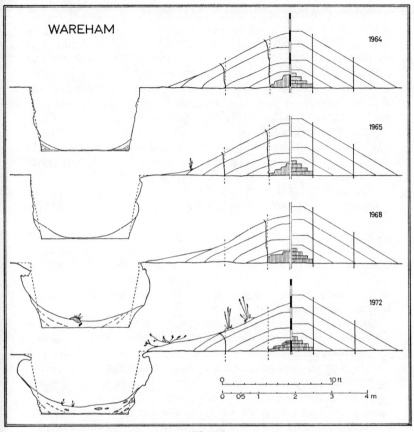

Fig. 13

Sections through experimental earthwork at Wareham, Dorset; original earthwork details on right (courtesy Brit. Assoc. Adv. Science, Exp. Earth. Comm.)

counter, and not merely the alterations occurring during a single lifetime. This is to a certain extent true, but the principle of experiment is at stake here, and without the effort there could be no results at all. The additions to our information about ditch silting are already extremely important, and those about the movement of material in an earthen bank are equally vital for the development of archaeological excavation techniques and interpretations.

Similar efforts, but of a more limited kind, have been made to record the construction and decay of other earthworks in Britain and abroad. After the excavation of Hollingbury Camp in Sussex, a sum of £4 was subscribed for the erection of posts in the post holes in order to gain some impression of the original appearance of the stockade. On Bindon Hill, Dorset, a 3-metre length of timber-laced earthen rampart was rebuilt after its excavation (Wheeler 1953); the timber and earth were provided, and the building operation took only one hour and 6 men. It was concluded that the whole defensive rampart could have been built in 16 days by 60 men, but the timber would have to be cut, and the earth scraped up for the bank, additional to this labour force. Similarly, at Stanwick, Yorkshire, 3 metres of the rampart revetment wall was built following its excavation (Wheeler 1954); the limestone bedrock here was easily broken in tabular slabs and estimates of time were again low. Yet the scale of this defensive system at Stanwick was quite considerable, and the whole operation must have involved a very large and well-directed labour force. The rampart was 13 metres wide, rested almost 7 metres above the base of a wide ditch, and had survived to a height of 3 metres. The raw materials were admirably suited to a structure of this character, and wedges and levers would have been the main implements required for the work.

Some of these reconstructions, and others (e.g. Burnez and Case 1966) attempted to rebuild only with the material believed to be collapsed from the structure; the results of this are not always reliable, however, as more recent quarrying of the debris, erosion of soils, and details of the possible organic framing are liable to be imponderables in most cases.

An experiment directed solely at the decay of the rampart, rather than its careful authentic reconstruction, was carried out in Scotland in 1937 (Childe and Thorneycroft 1938). One of the features of the Scottish Iron Age is the abundance of vitrified forts, defensive establishments the walls of which now consist of masses of fused basalts, with casts of timber beams within them. At Plean colliery, Stirlingshire, a 4-metre section of a rampart was built, 2 metres wide and 2 metres high (Fig. 14); it consisted of interlaced horizontal timbers with stone slabs and fireclay brick facings, and basalt rubble filling the body. The weight of the structure was well over 9 tonnes (9150 kg) of which the rubble weighed 7·5 tonnes and the timber 1·25 tonnes. The structure was ignited in a 20 mph snowstorm by 4 tonnes of heaped brushwood; the whole wall was burning fiercely in 30 minutes, and after 3 hours the outer and then the inner faces collapsed. The rubble became red hot at 5 hours and smouldered for 20 hours. After cooling, the wreck was excavated and the bottom rubble was found to have been vitrified into a solid mass. Part of the top rubble had also been melted, and droplets of rock were noted as well as the casts of some of the timbers that had been preserved

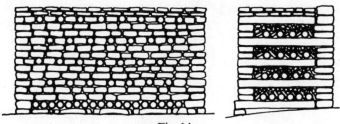

Fig. 14

Front face (*left*) and side view (*right*) of timber-laced wall at Plean, Stirlingshire (1/54) (after Childe and Thorneycroft 1938)

long enough to leave their imprint in the molten rock. The temperature achieved must have been at least 800°C, and possibly as much as 1200° C, for the basalt to melt. The conclusion of the experiment was that the vitrified forts of Scotland had originally had timber-laced ramparts filled out with basalt rubble, and had been accidentally set alight from interior huts set against the wall, or deliberately set alight from the exterior by attackers. The phenomenon of vitrifaction had been demonstrated.

At a time when timber-laced forts were being erected in northern Britain, Roman military turf-built forts were being constructed at quite incredible speed over parts of southern Britain. There has been much comment on the procedures used in the throwing-up of these defences, and recently an attempt has been made to achieve some precision in estimates of the time and labour involved. This took the form of a reconstruction of 11 metres of a Roman turf rampart at The Lunt, near Coventry, Warwickshire (Hobley 1967). The small fort here dates to the middle of the first century A.D., and was 91 × 61 metres in size. In 1966 part of the rampart was rebuilt with labour from Her Majesty's Prison, Leicester (Fig. 15).

The width of the rampart at its base was 5·4 metres, and there was no evidence of a vertical facing of timber or of timber-lacing within the rampart which had been placed at the extreme edge of an external ditch. The original height of the rampart was uncertain, but there must have been a fighting platform on the top of a width approaching 2 metres. This determined the shape of the

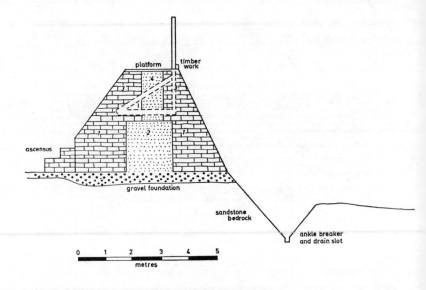

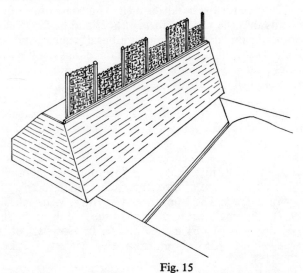

Fig. 15

Experimental turf rampart and ditch, The Lunt, Baginton, England:
above, section through rampart and ditch showing stages in building
the rampart; *below*, isometric view of the defences (from Hobley 1967)

rampart which required a facing slope of 65° and a height of 3·6 metres. The distance from ditch bottom to platform was a formidable 4·3 metres. The back of the rampart had a low vertical face, 1·2 metres high, as determined from other Roman forts, and then a sloped face at 45° leading up to the platform. Turf steps led up to the platform in one place.

The rampart as reconstructed was one-third earth fill, from the ditch, but the remainder was entirely turf. The turf was cut to prescribed Roman size, 1·5 × 1·0 × 0·5 Roman feet (44·4 × 29·6 × 14·8 cm), and laid grass to grass and earth to earth in horizontal courses. Each turf weighed from 32–4 kg and in the experiment it was found that 2 men were required to place the turf on the shoulders of the carrier who then transported it directly to the building site; in this way breakages due to over-handling were avoided. The turf was cut with saws and crescent-shaped blades such as are attested from Roman times, and the entire stock of turf was obtained from an area within 38 metres of the rampart. The stripping of the interior of the fort prior to building barracks, and perimeter areas, would have provided sufficient turf for the rampart.

For the 11 metre reconstruction, 5500–5750 turfs were needed including some broken turfs used as fill along with the earth. If the rampart had been built entirely of turf, then 7600 turfs were required. In any case, turf to a thickness of 2 metres at both front and rear of the rampart was required to resist the pressure from the internal filling; 1·4 metres of turf began to bulge during the experiment. The slight internal wooden framework, to hold up the vertical wall on the platform, also helped to support the earth fill.

The Lunt fort had a rampart 283 metres long, and this would require 138 000 turfs plus one-third earth fill, or 190 000 turfs without earth fill. The earth removed from the external ditch would save 12 400 turfs. In the rebuilding, 7–10 men working 6 hours per day completed the job in 20 days. The rate of turf-cutting, crucial for the work, was 4·5–6·5 turfs per man-hour. Roman records describe how centurions measured out the areas with 3·04 metre rods and each worker had his share allotted to him. If there had been 30 gangs of 7–10 men each, each gang putting up 10 metres of rampart, then about 210–300 men could have built the fort in 9–12 days if they worked a 10–hour day; the estimated garrison size of the Lunt is in fact about 300 men.

This experiment has enabled certain estimates of the rate of building by the Roman armies to be advanced with a good deal more confidence than previously seemed justifiable. The fort at

Chester, for example, with a huge rampart nearly 2000 metres long, needed about 2 million Roman turfs; half of its garrison of 5000 men could have built it in 12–14 days. The Antonine Wall across the midlands of Scotland, 59 km long and 4 metres wide, needed 26 million turfs, and could therefore have been built by a legion of 6000 men in 100 days; the feeding of such a body of men, and transportation facilities, would naturally have increased the size of party or the length of time involved in the exercise. Hadrian's Wall is slightly smaller.

The experimental reconstruction of the Lunt has been further advanced by the building of another 30 metres of rampart, 15 metres on each side of a reconstituted gateway (Pl. 8). The gateway, 9 metres high and with two doors each 3 metres wide, was designed from excavations here and elsewhere, from recorded Roman military data, and from representations on Trajan's Column. The rampart platform extends across the gateway with a tower built above to augment the defensive system. The wood used was pine rather than the oak employed by the Romans, and the gateway was erected in only 3 days by 25 Royal Engineers under the direction of Hobley.

Experiments such as these, in particular, the Overton Down earthwork, the vitrified fort, and the Roman turf rampart, have made major contributions to our knowledge of ancient building methods and have demonstrated not only the ease with which an organised labour force could accomplish feats of engineering, but the determination that must have been behind the planning and execution of structures as diverse as Avebury and the Antonine Wall.

TRANSPORT AND ERECTION OF STONES

Throughout both Old and New Worlds the traces of ancient man include evidence of his skill as an engineer in carving, transporting and erecting large stone monuments. Some of these lie unfinished in their quarries, some lie abandoned along their routes between quarry and destination, some lie in pieces around their original position, some still stand where they were raised. The fact that such stones occur throughout many areas of the world, and that they exhibit similar features in manufacture and movement, indicates a widespread interest of ancient man in such visually impressive monuments and his logical ingenuity in devising methods of handling such stones; the similarities do not themselves indicate any cultural or chronological relationship between areas.

The sizes of the stones vary, but the greatest of all was perhaps the granite obelisk at Aswan, unfinished and still resting in its quarry, 42 metres high and weighing 1168 tonnes. The Colossi of Memnon (Amenhotep III), on the plain of Thebes, weigh 1000 tonnes each. There are few other monuments to match these in weight, and none outside the ancient Near East. The stones of tombs at Mycenae weigh up to 120 tonnes, some of the megalithic tombs of western Europe have stones of over 100 tonnes, and the largest megalith in the west, the Grand Menhir Brisé in Brittany, is 382 tonnes. The stones at Avebury weigh up to 40 tonnes, and some Stonehenge sarsens weigh over 30 tonnes.

In the New World, the records are equally impressive (Heizer 1966). The largest in the New World, at Teotihuacan in Mexico, is an andesite statue weighing 217 tonnes. Olmec, Maya and Aztec sites all have stelae, altars or other blocks weighing around 20–60 tonnes, and some of the Inca fortress blocks weigh 200 tonnes or more. The statues on Easter Island in the Pacific are up to 60 tonnes.

All of these enormous stones had to be fashioned from the solid rock, and man-handled into place, and the transportation and erection of such material has always been a matter of great interest to archaeologists who are concerned to know more about the organisation of early societies. In only a few cases, however, have archaeologists taken the opportunity to experiment with ancient engineering procedures. The first of these processes is of course the actual shaping of the stones in the quarry. It is generally agreed that in the absence of modern metals, only the softest of rocks could have been cut, and the technique of carving hard rocks must have been with stone hammers, mauls and pounders; these would not cut but would either chip the rock or pulverise it into dust. The many unfinished statues and columns still lying in their quarries demonstrate these methods, and some have been reproduced experimentally.

The production of Egyptian obelisks was conducted by the use of dolerite balls weighing on average 5·5 kg; these were mounted as rammers and hurled or driven down onto the granite, powdering the stone (Engelbach 1923). By this, and by chisels and wedges, trenches were cut along the line of the obelisk and then joined by undercutting the monument to free it from the quarry. An experiment in the Aswan quarry showed that pounding of the granite for one hour reduced its level by 5 mm over the presumed work area of a stone mason; from this small test it was calculated that the Aswan obelisk could have been shaped and undercut in about

15 months by a team of 400 men, an upper team of 260 ramming the dolerite balls onto the rock, with 130 men in the trenches clearing away the cushioning dust. Egyptian records of the quarrying of the smaller Karnak obelisk suggests that 7 months were taken for the task; at the work rate experimentally estimated, the time would have been 9 months, so there is broad agreement. Yet the scale of the actual experiment was so small that multiplications of this order are highly suspect.

Six stone carvers of Easter Island, working with stone picks and mauls, and dampening the stone with water, probably could have shaped a 5-metre statue in about one year. A small experiment was carried out on the Island within the quarry of Rano-Raraku, and this showed that definite work areas for each man were required, and that one of the largest statues, 21 metres long, would have accommodated no more than 30 men, 15 on each side (Skjolsvold 1961).

Estimates for the dressing, not quarrying, of the sarsen uprights of Stonehenge show the amount of effort that must have been required to prepare these stones, of a type that is said to be 2 or 3 times as hard to work as granite. It is calculated that 50 masons working 10 hours a day, all year round, would have taken almost 3 years to dress the stones by pounding and grinding. Experimental work here could profitably be undertaken.

Of more general interest, and certainly an aspect demonstrating the organisation of labour in ancient times, are those experiments concerned with the transport and erection of stone monuments. The scale of the exercise may be judged by representations in reliefs and paintings of the transportation of heavy objects in Egypt and the Middle East. One of these records the movement of an alabaster statue, 7 metres high, of Prince Djehutihetep of Egypt (Fig. 16). The detail in the relief suggests, but does not prove, that the quantities of workers depicted are likely to be accurate indications of the amount of labour required to move this enormous statue which may have weighed as much as 60 tonnes. The statue is tied to a wooden sledge which is being dragged along by 90 men hauling on ropes. The overseer stands on the knee of the statue and beats time, 'heave' and 'rest' with his hands; the sound is enhanced by a man with wooden clappers. Another man pours water in front of the sledge to reduce friction, and is supplied by 3 water carriers. Three men cart a wooden beam for easing the sledge over bumps. At the back are 3 overseers with sticks, and 12 reserves. Possibly as essential for the continued progress of the sledge are 6 groups of 10 soldiers with whips and clubs. The total

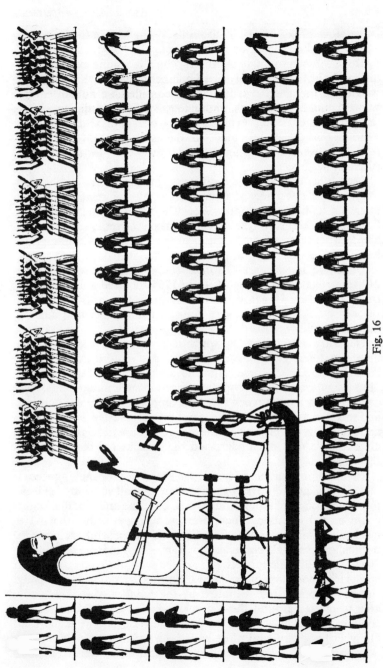

Fig. 16

Ancient transport of a stone statue in Egypt

is therefore 174, of which 99 are actively engaged in the work, the others providing encouragement. This supplies us with an estimated figure of 99 men to move 60 tonnes which is a quite exceptionally and probably unacceptably small number of men for such a heavy weight. In any case, it is likely that considerable human energy was expended upon such monuments, if we can disregard the fairly consistent local explanations, from both Old and New Worlds, that the stones could will themselves to move and those resting between quarry and destination were *piedras cansadas* (tired stones).

The difficulties of using ordinary human effort upon such weights and sizes may also be gauged by the relatively recent attempts to move and raise ancient stone monuments pillaged from the Near East. Layard's comments on the removal of the bull and lion sculptures from Nimrud to the Tigris indicate the problems, as does the erection of a 510-tonne obelisk in Rome with 907 men, 75 horses and 40 windlasses; even the movement of a 217-tonne statue to Mexico City in 1964 required a 112-wheeled trailer pulled by 4 tractors, at least an indication of the weight of the object. All of these were transported in ancient times by human labour.

There are several ways by which heavy stones could have been moved without elaborate machinery. All require exceptionally large human labour forces, and this simple fact is the reason behind the interest shown by prehistorians in such monuments. The collection of a large work force presupposes economic, political and social organisation on a scale not otherwise often documented, and adds appreciably to our knowledge of human behaviour even although we may not understand the reasons for the structures themselves.

The methods that could have been employed for moving stones in antiquity are by carrying, by water, by rollers or by sledges. For the raising of stones, ramps, pits, or stone and wooden cribs, could have been used. There are several experiments that have tried to demonstrate the suitability of these general methods in particular situations, but a case can be made for more experimental work with full-scale models.

The transportation of stones by lifting and carrying is a relatively simple operation, but is limited by the number of men actually able to cluster around the object. At La Venta, Mexico, basalt columns for an Olmec site of the first millennium B.C. were quarried about 80km away, and must have been rafted to a point where they could be dragged or carried to their destination. An experiment in 1955 showed that a column of 2 tonnes was the maximum which could be lifted by 35 men using rope slings and shoulder poles (Drucker, Heizer and Squier 1959). The largest stele on the site weighs 50 tonnes and, at a lifting ratio of 100 kg per man, this would require 500 men; it would not be possible for 500 men to arrange themselves in lifting positions for a column only 4 metres long, even with pole-carriers, and the large stones therefore must have been dragged. In Colombia, a team of 35 men managed to lift and carry a stone sculpture weighing one tonne over 7 km in a week, cutting a trail through forest as they went. Sixty Nepalese men carrying a litter bearing a Mercedes car, weight 1·5 tonnes, would make a fair comparison.

For stones or objects weighing over 2 tonnes, it is likely that dragging over land would be the normal method of transport, but however this was organised, there can be no doubt that movement by water was far easier in terms of human energies. Egyptian wall reliefs depict the transport of obelisks, weighing well over 300 tonnes, in lighters pulled by small vessels down the Nile. The loading of such heavy objects was accomplished by floating weighted lighters into a canal dug under the central part of the stone; then the vessels were unloaded and so rose and eventually lifted the obelisk clear of the ground supports. Rafts were also used to transport the bull figures that eventually were placed in Nineveh; these weighed about 30 tonnes each, and were mounted on sledges at the quarry, then moved en masse onto rafts on the Tigris.

An experiment in the transportation of monoliths by water was carried out on the River Avon near Stonehenge, England (Atkinson 1956). The stones of Stonehenge include the famous bluestones, quarried in the Prescelly mountains of south Wales and transported by sea and river and land over a distance of 240 km. A replica of one of these bluestones, weighing just under 2 tonnes, was crane-loaded onto wooden planks over 3 canoes. The craft was easily manipulated by 4 schoolboys with poles up river, and the total weight of about 2 tonnes drew only 23 cm of water; it could have been poled up very shallow creeks and streams. No experiments were carried out to see if this form of craft could have withstood the waters of the Bristol Channel and the estuary of the Severn.

Most megalithic monuments do not lie immediately adjacent to waterways, and land transport was essential. Contrary to belief, the use of wooden rollers is not attested in the archaeological record, and experiments have shown that rollers are not very successful unless the ground is quite even and firm. Extremely heavy weights might well crush the rollers. The Stonehenge experiments, however, showed that the bluestone replica, mounted on a wooden sledge, could be moved by a team of about 12 men with a further 12 to collect and place the rollers in position in front of the advancing sledge.

The use of sledges, in fact, was without doubt the most popular method adopted in the ancient world for the overland transport of heavy stones. Representations from Egypt and the Middle East show in detail the shape of sledges and the various tasks that the human labourers had to carry out to ease their passage over the ground; the organisation of effort to move Prince Djehutihetep's statue has already been described.

Recent observations of the transport of heavy stones by groups of people in south-east Asia and elsewhere have confirmed the widespread use of sledges. In Sumba, an 11-tonne block was dragged on a sledge by 552 men for a distance of 3 km before being hauled up a log ramp into place as a tomb capstone (Heizer 1966).

The Stonehenge experiment also tested the use of sledge-transport without rollers. The sledge was made of 15 cm square timbers and measured 2·7 × 1·2 metres. The weight of sledge and stone was just under 2 tonnes, and this was dragged over firm ground and up slopes of 4° (1 in 15) by 32 schoolboys (Atkinson 1956). It was calculated that at a work-load rating of 16 men per tonne weight, 110 men would have been needed to drag the largest of the bluestones on a similar sledge. The sarsen uprights of the great outer circle at Stonehenge weigh 25 tonnes each, and the central sarsens are perhaps 40 tonnes each. These came from the Marlborough Downs, 32 km away, and would have required huge sledges with or without rollers; at 22 men per tonne weight, 40 tonne stones would need 880 men who might have managed one kilometre a day. Beyond this the conjecture grows more and more uncertain, but the 81 sarsens on these calculations occupied perhaps 1500 men for 5 years full time. The magnitude of the labour and time, however it is permutated, is quite enormous and perhaps enhanced by the knowledge that this work was carried out some 4000 years ago.

A similar experiment in moving stone by sledge was carried out in 1956 on Easter Island (Heyerdahl 1958; Skjolsvold 1961). The remarkable series of human figures lying unfinished in the quarries of the volcano Rano-Raraku, lying abandoned in the earth or toppled from their stone platforms, have been considered to exhibit strong similarities with carved figures from coastal South

America and form a small part of the theory that links Easter Island and the Society Islands to the west through colonisation from the Americas (Heyerdahl 1952).

Some of the Easter Island figures are 9 metres tall and weigh up to 50 tonnes, but many are smaller. Some were carved with a tapered base for erection in the earth, others had flat bases for positioning on stone platforms and sometimes had reddish stone cylinders placed on top of the heads. The statues are densely distributed around the volcanic quarry, but some were transported as much as 10 km. Local legend in the island states that the statues moved themselves under orders from a chieftain with supernatural powers, but Heyerdahl's experimental transportation of a statue relied upon 180 local men hauling on 2 ropes attached to a sledge made of a forked tree stem. The statue lashed to the sledge weighed 10–12 tonnes, and was 4 metres long. It was pointed out that an alternative method of moving the figures was by placing them upon their convex stomachs and wedging and rocking them along; this would account for the legend that they had 'walked' to their places.

The erection of tall stone monuments, whether they be the undressed uprights of Avebury, the dressed sarsens of Stonehenge, the carved obelisks of Egypt or the human figures of the New World, presents little difficulty in terms of technique if they are to be supported in pits. Where these monuments were placed upon stone platforms, the *ahu* of Easter Island, then greater difficulties arise. There have been several experiments concerned with the erection of stones in pits dug either into the ground or into artificial mounds built over stone bases. Both of those described here were scaled experiments and their results are therefore perhaps not as valid as they might have been.

The erection of Egyptian obelisks in modern times has been fraught with problems, and has involved much manpower and machinery; the splintering of the wooden cribbing beneath the New York obelisk is a case in point. The heaviest single stone monument in the world perhaps is the unfinished Aswan obelisk weighing 1168 tonnes. Others weigh 400 tonnes or more, and a model to demonstrate the erection of one of these was described in 1923 (Engelbach 1923); the model was at a scale of 1/1000, and the exercise was to place an obelisk upon a stone platform at about ground level. A ramp of earth and stones was built around the platform, so that the obelisk could be dragged base first upwards to lie well above the platform. Within the ramped deposit there was a funnel-shaped hole partly filled with sand and covering the platform. As the obelisk was dragged upwards, its base over-hung the funnel until the point of balance was over-reached; it then tipped down into the funnel and was halted by the sand. The judicious removal of sand through a slit-like exit at the base of the funnel allowed the obelisk to slide further and further down until it came eventually to rest upon the platform. We may suspect that in actual operation it may not have been as simple, but the method appears sound. Alternative procedures with shearlegs and levers would also be possible in some but not all cases where obelisks were erected in confined places.

A larger-scaled experiment was concerned with the erection of the sarsen uprights of Stonehenge (Stone 1924). The sarsens of this monument weigh up to 40 tonnes and are up to 9 metres tall. A model of one of these sarsens at a scale of 1/12 was constructed, and was positioned on rollers lying upon carefully prepared level ground (Fig. 17). A hole was dug to receive the base of the stone, with a sloping ramp of 45° facing the stone and a vertical face opposite. The stone was then rolled gently forward until it over-balanced and tipped into the hole, coming to rest on the 45° angle of the ramp. A pair of shearlegs were placed in position on the opposite side of the hole, and a crossbar was lashed to the top of the stone. Ropes joined this to the shearlegs so that the pull on the rope was at right angles to the plane of the stone. The shear-legs were raised by hauling on ropes attached to the top and gradu-ally the stone was lifted to a vertical position when it could be packed with stones.

Calculations were made on the basis of this experiment that a 26-tonne stone would require a pull at the top of the shearlegs of 4·5 tonnes. The effective pull of a man on a rope is ·025 (1/40) tonne, so it would require 180 men to raise the stone to a vertical position. This seems an entirely reasonable proposition, and the archaeological evidence from Stonehenge itself does not contradict the proposed method (Atkinson 1956).

The scaled experiment continued with attempts to place the lintels on top of the upright sarsens. The sarsens of the outer circle extend to 4 metres above the ground, and those of the inner group are uneven, the top of the largest being 7 metres above the ground. Each outer circle sarsen was joined to its neighbours by stone lintels held in place through mortice and tenon, each up-right having two tenons. The lintels were carved with a tongue at one end, a groove at the other, and two mortice holes on one broad face.

Three methods for lifting and positioning the lintels onto the

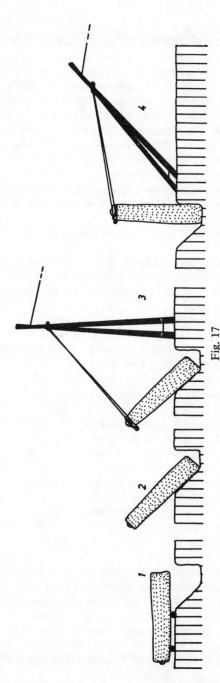

Fig. 17

Stages in the erection of one of the sarsens at Stonehenge, England, according to the scale model of Stone (1924)

uprights have been proposed. One of these involves the building of a large earthen bank around each pair of uprights, with a smooth outer ramp leading to the top, and two vertical posts within the bank to hold ropes. The scale model constructed to demonstrate the method had wooden rollers bound onto the lintel faces, and wooden bearers lying on top of the bank on either side of the tenons of the upright stones. Ropes were tied to the wooden bollard posts, looped beneath the bearers, down the ramp, twice around the bound lintel, up the ramp and over the bearers or bolsters onto the inner side of the circle of stones. The pull on the ropes would then parbuckle the lintel up the bank, turning it over and over. The ropes would have to be greased to reduce friction.

The amount of manpower required to move the lintel in this way was calculated on the basis that half the weight of the lintel, about 7 tonnes, would be taken by the bollards, the other half by the actual pull on the ropes. About 100–150 men would be able to raise the lintel in this way. At the top, the use of rollers and levers would allow the lintel to be manoeuvred into the tongue or grooves of the adjacent lintel, and over the tenons of the uprights. The model experiment demonstrated that a handful of men could have done this. The removal of the bank and its ramp would then have followed and the task was done.

The basis for the use of a large ramp at Stonehenge lies in the acknowledged practice of building long ramps for the raising of stone monuments in Egypt. A scaled model of the building of the third pyramid of the Giza group has demonstrated the procedures involved although no actual experiment was conducted (Dunham 1956). This pyramid, constructed about 2600 B.C. for King Mycerinus, was composed of multiple courses of red granite quarried at the First Cataract and transported by barge, and white limestone from the Tura quarries moved by barge across the Nile valley during the inundations. The blocks were then dragged to an assembly area near the site of the pyramid. No wheeled vehicles were available, nor were there draught animals, so all the labour was human.

On the basis of surviving evidence, mostly fragmentary, the model pyramid was constructed to show that one method for moving the blocks ever upwards, as the pyramid grew, was to build earth and stone ramps, at a slope of 1 in 8, attached to the sides of the pyramid. The casing blocks of the pyramid were left rough until the final dressing which was carried out from the top and this rough casing would have allowed the erection of a 3-metre wide ramp stuck onto the side of the pyramid. The model suggested that a ramp could have been started from each corner, so that 3 ramps could have been used for transport of blocks, and 1 for the return of men and empty sledges down to get another block. It was calculated that the use of sledges, with water, would allow relatively easy movement upwards particularly if the ramp roads had been strengthened and smoothed by transverse logs. The passage of sledges around the corners would have entailed upright posts to carry the rope strain at right angles, and levers to manipulate the sledges. The model constructed presumed to show only how the pyramid might have been made, and no proof is forthcoming. It did, however, dispose of Herodotus' claim that it had taken 100000 men to build the Great Pyramid; the model, fully occupied by teams, held only 2500 men and it was thought that the site could not have accommodated many more. The addition of quarrymen and bargemen and hauliers, and perhaps too the people who fed and sheltered all of those engaged in the great work, might well increase the total by a substantial factor.

This use of ramps is of course on a different scale from that at Stonehenge. Surviving remains of ramps do exist in Egypt, and their value in such mammoth undertakings is clear. Objections against the use of the Stonehenge ramp for raising the lintels are on the basis of the time involved in building and moving earthen ramps from upright to upright, and the fact that no quarry for the material has been recognised; the previously existing outer bank and ditch were not reused in the operation of lifting the lintels. Of the other two methods which could have been adopted at Stonehenge, neither has been attempted in experiments. The first is the construction of a timber ramp instead of an earthen one, but no post holes for this have been recognised in the excavations. The second is the use of a wooden crib, and this has the merit of simplicity, easy assembly and dismantling, and absence of any necessity for archaeologically recognisable post holes (Atkinson 1956).

The timber crib postulated for Stonehenge is of some interest as it is the same principle as that used in full-scale experiments on Easter Island. The Stonehenge crib would consist of a series of wooden beams and planks. The stone would be levered up at one end and a bearer inserted. The other end would then be levered up and another bearer put beneath it. In this way each end could be raised and the stone uplifted to any required height. The force required to raise one end of a 6- or 7-tonne stone, using a 4-metre lever with a fulcrum 30cm from its end, would require 7 men each exerting 45 kg pressure. To allow these men to operate, and subsequently to level the lintel sideways onto the uprights, some form of platform would be required and this could be provided at stages between the bearer piles; in fact the provision of such platforms would stabilise the timbers of the crib. Ropes would of course be attached to the ends of the levers, and only one or two men would be required on the crib to position the levers. About 1·6 km of 15 × 15 cm timber would be needed, in lengths of about 6 metres.

The ease with which such a timber crib would function would probably exceed that of a stone-built crib such as was tested on Easter Island (Heyerdahl 1958; Skjolsvold 1961). Of the many statues on the island, none was still in place upon its *ahu* or stone platform, and an experiment was mounted to see how difficult it would be actually to raise the largest fallen statue and place it upon its *ahu*. The statue weighed about 25 tonnes and lay face down in the earth. A team of 12 men from the island started work with three wooden levers and many stone slabs for use as wedges. By levering up one side and then the other, and by wedging in stones along the entire length of the figure, the statue was raised to a horizontal position over 3 metres above the ground and firmly held upon the heap of stones. By levering judiciously, the men hanging upon ropes, the base of the statue was gradually shifted near the *ahu*. After 11 days' work, the stone wedges were placed only beneath the head and chest of the figure, which gradually rose until it was balanced at almost 45°, its base pointing towards the *ahu* beneath. Ropes were then tied to the statue, some held by men, others wound round a post, and a final leverage put into motion. The statue slid down the piled stones and came to rest upon the *ahu*. The whole operation had occupied 12 men for 18 days.

The point was immediately grasped that the reddish stone *pukao* or topknots, still in place upon some of the statues during Cook's visit in 1777, and weighing up to 20 tonnes, could have been manoeuvred up the rebuilt pile of stones and onto the head of the statue if required. The experiment did not extend to this, however, and it only remained to dismantle the stone heap and leave the statue in place. The experiment had been extraordinarily simple yet required very considerable expertise and judgment.

A group of experiments in digging and transporting earth and stone, and in masonry processes, thus bringing together many observations, was carried out in Mexico (Erasmus 1965) in an attempt to discover the amount of effort needed to build the Maya ceremonial centre at Uxmal, near Tikul. This centre, covering an area 1200×600 metres, has been estimated to contain 850000 cubic metres of fill (earth and stone) and to have been built and used for a relatively short period of time of about 250 years.

The experiments were small in scale but carefully recorded, and were based upon a 5-hour working day in this area from about 0600 to 1100 hours by which time the temperatures had risen from an early morning 30°C to 43°C. Tests showed that a sixth hour of work in open sun was unproductive and greatly lowered the average energy output of the natives.

The experiments began with the excavation and carriage of earth, and for the latter, both shovels and digging sticks were used. The contest between these, designed to last for several hours, was enlivened by a promise of piece-work rates, 'but the speed of their work so exceeded my expectations that I had to halt the experiment after thirty minutes' (Erasmus 1965, 285). The shovel was found to be about 2·5 times as efficient as the digging stick plus hands. The earth was transported in 5-gallon cans by two carriers, one covering 50 metres, the other 100 metres. Their performances, over 5 hours, appear in the table below:

EARTH CARRIAGE (5-HOUR DAY)

	Distance per trip m	Total trips	Total distance km	Total weight kg	Total volume m³
I	50	206	20·6	4151	3·17
II	100	116	23·2	2313	1·76

Many of the monumental structures at Uxmal are of stone, and experiments were conducted in both quarrying and carriage of local limestones, a crucial series for estimates of time. Again, modern and ancient implements were in contest, in this case an iron crowbar and a hardwood pole, for prising out blocks of stone. Maya Indians who had experience of this were employed, and their rate of achievement was incredibly fast. In the 5-hour day 5000 kg of rock were levered with the metal crowbar from an area about 30 square metres in size, and this was about 3 times as much as the wooden crowbar could produce. The rock came away as large lumps, about 25 kg in weight, and 200 of these were dislodged by the metal tool in the working day.

Four men were then employed to carry some of these lumps over distances from 250 m to 1 km. Two of the men (A and C in the table,) were 'pure' Maya, the others were not; all carried the rocks by a tumpline, except one man (A) who balanced the rocks on his head.

ROCK CARRIAGE (5 HOUR DAY)

	Distance per trip m	Total trips	Total distance km	Total weight kg	Weight per trip kg
A	250	34	17	950	28
B	500	20	20	500	25
C	750	15	22·5	517	34
D	1 km	11	22	250	23

The average distance travelled was 21 km, of which half was with a load of about 25 kg or heavier. Man A travelled less far because the first 100 m of the route, representing a large percentage of his total trip, was over uneven ground, he had to balance the rock on his head, and he spent proportionately more time loading than the others.

The results of these experiments, when applied to Uxmal, suggested a total of 4·5 million man-days required to obtain and bring earth and stone to the centre; the site contained 0·85 million cubic metres of fill weighing 1·3 million tonnes of earth and rock obtainable from an area of 7·5 million square metres. The average distance required to transport this material was 750 m, at a carriage rate of 500 kg per man-day.

The next set of tests for the site concerned stone masonry, and a test wall was built by a Maya mason with the 517 kg of rock carried by man C. The building of 1 cubic metre of masonry took 4 days and 1400 kg rock, 100 kg lime, and 300 kg *sascab* (a local replacement for sand in mortar, and readily available by shallow mining). Estimates, not experiments, were made of lime burning, *sascab* mining, and these figures were then applied to the 0·4 million cubic metres of masonry at Uxmal to yield 0·5 million man-days. Finally, the cutting and sculpturing of the limestone façades were tested by experiment; it took the mason about 3 man-days to plain veneer or shallow sculpture an area of masonry 1000 square centimetres (0·1 × 1·0 m), and for the ·075 million square metres of cut stone at Uxmal, this meant 2·5 million man-days.

The grand total for the basic building techniques at Uxmal, quarrying, transporting, and building, is estimated at 7·5 million man-days. Granted a period of interest in the site of 250 years, this is an average 30000 man-days per year for ceremonial constructions. Population densities for the area do not fall within the

experimental aspect, but the whole purpose of the exercise was to deduce the required output per family for ceremonial works, and so some note should be made here of the final figures. At a modest 8·5 hectares per family, $\frac{1}{2}$ of the fields fallow, and an 8 km territorial range, $\frac{1}{2}$ of this cultivable, the area would support 1200 families; each of these could perhaps spare the adult male for 40 days each year for public buildings and works, so the total available would have been 48000 man-days over 250 years, well able to cope with the building programme. At a better guess, ceremonial building in short more intensive bursts would have allowed the erection of the largest monument at Uxmal, requiring ·65 million man-days, in only 7 years if we doubled the annual effort per family. The whole operation was readily within the capabilities of the Maya community, judged by agricultural and building experiments and observations.

Although we may wonder at the immensity of all these monuments, Uxmal, Stonehenge, Easter Island and so on, experimental work surely shows that only the simplest of machinery and techniques were required for even the most elaborate of these structures. This should not reduce their importance in our eyes, because the monuments, and our knowledge of them gained through experiments, demonstrate more than anything else the organisation of ancient man, the gathering together, permanently or temporarily, of large work forces united in common desire.

BOATS AND VOYAGES

The movement of monoliths is not the only achievement of ancient man in the field of transport. The colonisation of many areas of the world only took place at a time when sea levels were such that some passage across open water was necessary. The occupation of Australia and New Zealand are obvious examples of long-distance travel at separate times, and although the shortest crossing to Australia from New Guinea is only 200 kilometres, the waters of relatively narrow straits are perhaps more dangerous than greater expanses of open water, the 500 km between Indonesia and Australia for example. The distances to New Zealand from Melanesia or from Australia are appreciably greater, yet these distances were achieved in the past by a range of ocean-going craft that to our eyes might have appeared totally incapable of such feats. The *Kon-Tiki* expedition was the first to be publicised of a series of journeys that have demonstrated the effectiveness of ancient forms of craft in open ocean conditions.

The theory behind the voyage in the *Kon-Tiki* was that parts of Polynesia could have been colonised from America; archaeologically, it was believed that the similarities between the ancient cultures of coastal South America and those of Polynesia were sufficient to support the idea of a common society. One of the stumbling blocks in the idea was the lack of conviction on the part of almost every archaeologist that any ocean-going craft known to exist in these early times was capable of withstanding the long journey, and that the oceanic currents and winds would have carried the vessels to Polynesia. It was to test these two aspects that the *Kon-Tiki* expedition was mounted (Heyerdahl 1950).

The type of craft chosen to make the test was a Peruvian raft of balsa wood, considered to represent accurately the ancient Inca form of ocean-going raft. The raft was made of nine trunks of balsa wood felled in the interior forests of Peru and floated down-river to the port of Callao. The logs were grooved to hold hemp rope bindings, and were tied together to make a raft about 14 metres long and 5 metres wide. The logs were uneven in length, the longest placed at the centre line, and together they formed a pointed raft with a blunt stern bearing a balsa block for the steering oar.

On top of the raft logs were laid thinner logs at intervals of about one metre, to carry a deck of split bamboo covered by loose mats of plaited bamboo reeds. Near the middle of the raft was a cabin built of bamboo cane with reed walls and a roof of bamboo slats and banana leaf tiles. Two mangrove wood masts were set forward of the cabin, their upper ends lashed together. A square canvas sail, 5×6 metres, was hauled up on a yard of 2 bamboo stems bound together. The balsa logs of the raft were about half submerged, and slender balsa logs were put along the sides for protection from the sea and to prevent loss of cargo and men. The uneven nature of the logs caused large gaps between them, and these were filled with pine planks wedged and tied to project about 1·5 metres into the water; these acted as keels and centreboards to prevent the craft drifting sideways.

The finished raft was pronounced unsuitable for ocean travel by almost all who saw her in the port of Callao. All agreed she would not complete the voyage, but it could not be decided if the reason for failure would be the logs breaking, the ropes breaking, the logs sinking, or the crew being washed overboard.

On 28 April 1947, the *Kon-Tiki* was towed 80 km out to sea into the Humboldt Current, and started its voyage to the west. Great difficulty was experienced at first in steering the raft; a mangrove wood steering pole, 6 metres long, had a pine oar blade strapped to it, the pole resting between 2 pins in the balsa block at the stern of the vessel. Ropes also secured the pole to the sides of the raft allowing it to move but not to be displaced by the very severe strains put on it by the sea. The steering watch consisted of 2 men at first, later one, and the main task was to keep the stern of the raft into the wind and current.

Heavy seas were no real problem, as the water thrown onto the raft merely flowed away between the logs; a boat would surely have foundered. The logs became water-softened but only for about 3 cm thickness, the sap in the fresh wood preventing deeper water-logging. The ropes tended to bite further into the logs as the wood softened, and this prevented fraying. It was found that by raising and lowering the pine centreboards, the course of the raft could be altered. The average number of kilometres sailed per day was 79, but some progress was made on every day, the minimum being 16 km, the maximum over 130.

Military rations had been taken in sufficient quantities for 6 men for 4 months, and 250 gallons of water as well. There was no difficulty in obtaining food from the sea, and a constant stream of flying fish, bonitos and dolphin was consumed. Fresh water was not in short supply either, as extra sources could be found in rainfall, and liquid could be squeezed from fishmeat. After 45 days, 3700 km had been covered, and on 17 July, island seabirds were sighted. The currents carried the raft past the island of Angatau at the end of July, although the islanders attempted to tow the *Kon-Tiki* into the lagoon. On 7 August the raft was washed into the Raroia reef, and the cabin and masts were wrecked by waves, but all hands were safe, and the crew happily occupied a small island behind the reef until taken off by ship.

The bare recital of facts about the *Kon-Tiki* expedition disguise the very real drama and adventure in this bold attempt to test a theory by experiment. The results, of course, did not prove that Polynesia was settled from America, but they showed that a South American balsa raft could have survived long enough in the sea to complete the voyage of over 6400 km, and that the currents and the winds were suitable for such an exploration; the strength and direction of these currents and winds make it likely that once the voyage started, deliberately or accidentally, there was no turning back.

Among the various voyages across the Pacific since *Kon-Tiki*, a recent (1970) expedition extends the range of balsa rafts dramatically. A 7-log raft with 2 masts and a cabin was successfully

guided across the Pacific, from Ecuador to a reef 129 km north of
Brisbane, Australia. The crew of 4 had as much fresh water left
as it had started with, and there were no problems over food
supplies. The raft, *La Balsa*, had sailed 13 700 km in 22 weeks, in
a successful attempt by her Spanish captain, Vital Alzar, to show
again that the major Pacific island groups were within reach of
South America. The basic difficulty with these theories of colonisation from America is that the experiments prove only that one-
way voyages were possible, while round trips allowing prepared
colonising expeditions are clearly impossible.

Not all of the experiments concerned with Pacific island colonisation have concentrated upon such long-distance voyages. The
islands of Polynesia alone cover well over 3000 km and inter-
island settlement and communication is an equally important
aspect of this region. Several experiments have been conducted
with a view to establishing the potential of Polynesian boats for
inter-island colonisation.

The longest reputed voyages within Polynesia are those between
the Hawaiian Islands on the one hand and the Marquesas and the
Society Islands on the other. A current archaeological view is that
Hawaii was discovered and colonised from the Marquesas, and
subsequently contact was made with the Society Islands. The
question arose whether or not it was possible for Polynesians to
construct and sail a boat over these long distances, well over
3200 km. Accidental or one-way voyages were presumed to have
occurred, but deliberate exploration, report and colonisation were
thought to be outside the capabilities of early Polynesians. The
arguments for this view were that their craft could not be sailed
to windward and would break up in heavy seas, the navigators
could not locate and find the remote islands, and the currents and
winds were too unpredictable.

Two experiments have been carried out to test some of these
beliefs. The Polynesian double canoe was considered to be the
most suitable long-distance open water craft, and although no
direct evidence of the type in use from the first to the fourteenth
century A.D. exists, observations during the last three centuries,
and the wide distribution of a particular form, suggested that the
early double canoe was probably both a sailing and paddling craft,
with a low freeboard and a spit sail (Fig. 18). Hawaiian canoes were
considered to be close copies of the original Polynesian canoes,
and this form was used in the experiments. Three questions were
asked: (1) could such canoes sail to windward? (2) could such
canoes make headway by paddling alone? (3) could such canoes

Fig. 18
Double canoes from *a*, New Caledonia; *b*, Belep Islands

withstand heavy seas? Answers to the first two questions were obtained.

The Hawaiian double canoe was up to 20 metres long, and carried as many as 80 men according to records. The hulls were not decked over, and the freeboard was low, perhaps 60 cm. The hulls were linked by 6 cross-pieces, 4 main and 1 each at bow and stern. A narrow platform was built over the cross-pieces between the hulls, leaving room for inboard paddlers. One or two masts were lashed to the platform, and carried woven pandanus sails of triangular shape with the apex held down to a curved boom. Large steering paddles were held against the hulls near the stern.

The first experiment used small models to test if such canoes could sail into the wind (Bechtol 1963). Various shapes of hull were tested on 75 cm models, and different widths of steering paddles were used. Canoes with V-sharp or rounded hulls could sail within 45° of the wind with large steering paddles, only within 60–80° of the wind with small paddles. The conclusion was that

Polynesians would not be able to sail closer to the wind than about 70° or 80°.

A more accurate estimate of the capabilities of Polynesian double canoes was obtained by a further experiment using a full-size canoe (Finney 1967). A replica double canoe was built of fibreglass, moulded from a Hawaiian outrigger; the hulls were 12 metres long, with maximum depth 1 metre and beam 60 cm. The hulls were held 1·1 metres apart by 6 cross-pieces supporting a platform. The total weight of the vessel was 1360 kg, slightly more than a similar double canoe built with Hawaiian materials would have weighed. The replica was not suitable for testing the strength of Polynesian canoes in heavy seas. However, it was found in a series of experiments carried out off the Californian coast and in the Hawaiian islands that the double canoe could sail downwind at 8 knots in a moderate wind, could sail crosswind (90°) at 6 knots, and, most important, could sail at 75° to windward at 4–5 knots in the same conditions. It made little windward headway in very light airs. A larger steering paddle, and V-sharp hull, might have improved windward performance.

A further experiment was carried out using a crew of 12 men in a paddling exercise (Finney 1967; Horvath and Finney 1969). Over 2 days, 84 km were paddled with 8 men, 2 reserves and 2 steersmen, in the canoe which fully-laden weighed 3 tonnes. A maximum racing speed of 6 knots was achieved, but a rate of 3 knots was averaged in calm conditions over 8-hour stretches. Against wind and current, however, progress was very slow and difficult; only one knot was reached in a slight current and 20 knot headwind, and in open water, a heavy sea would probably have halted all progress. It was considered that about 40 km per day was possible for an 8-hour row, but if more paddling was required then a reserve crew and a larger heavier boat would be needed. In doldrum conditions, however, paddling was clearly possible, although the food and water requirements would be high.

With these results it was possible to estimate the potential value of such canoes in the discovery and colonisation of Polynesia (Fig. 19). Using known factors of winds and currents, it could be shown to be impossible for the Hawaiian Islands to have been reached from either the Society or Marquesas Islands by drifting, that is, by a canoe lost at sea and not purposefully sailing into the wind. By sailing for about 20 days, at only 105° to the wind, Hawaii could have been reached from the Marquesas, but the return journey would have involved sailing within 65° to the wind and this was not possible experimentally. The voyage from Tahiti and the Society Islands to Hawaii would also be relatively easy, involving sailing at 95° to the wind for the 4000 km, and the return journey at 75° also was within the capabilities of the canoe, the voyage taking about 30 days.

The island blocks of Polynesia are extremely large, the Society Islands measuring 250 × 460 km, the Hawaiian islands three times this size, and so navigation problems would not be insuperable. In any case, the extraordinary skill exhibited by various Polynesian sailors in locating their positions accurately while voyaging between the islands, using a combination of factors involving stars, sun, wind, currents, sea birds, cloud formations, and swells of the sea, suggest that no difficulty need have been experienced in navigation in the past (Lewis 1972). The problems of human survival seem surmountable in terms of food and drink, judged by Heyerdahl's and Alzar's journeys. No experimental data on the seaworthiness of the double canoe are available.

The conclusions of these extremely useful experiments are that if Hawaii was settled from the Marquesas and Society Islands, both were by planned exploration and were not by accidental one-way drift. Return journeys to the Society Islands were possible to allow colonisation voyages to be arranged. The direct return journey to the Marquesas was not possible but by sailing at 75° to the wind the canoes could reach Tuamoto and then sail eastwards to the Marquesas when occasional suitable winds permitted. We must remain impressed by the potential abilities of the Polynesian double canoe for open-water travel of over 3200 km, although again it is to be emphasised that the fact that it can be done is no proof that it was done. This addition to archaeological knowledge is, however, of very great importance in that it allows evidence for contact to be assessed under the heading of 'possible' rather than 'impossible'.

A more recent experiment was also concerned with the reconstruction of a vessel from early records, its testing, and relation to another long-distance traveller, in this case Odysseus (Tilley 1971). The ship of Odysseus is shown on a fifth-century vase now in the British Museum; Odysseus is bound to the mast, the crew are rowing stolidly with ears no doubt filled with beeswax, and off-stage the music of the sirens can be imagined. The problem is not the music but the oarsmen, because only 4 are shown although 6 oars are clearly visible. The suggestion has been made that the vessel was propelled by 12 men, 6 oars each side, 3 men to a bench. Odysseus' ship has a ram and is therefore a warship or one engaged in piracy, and the provision of 3 oars per bench would increase its

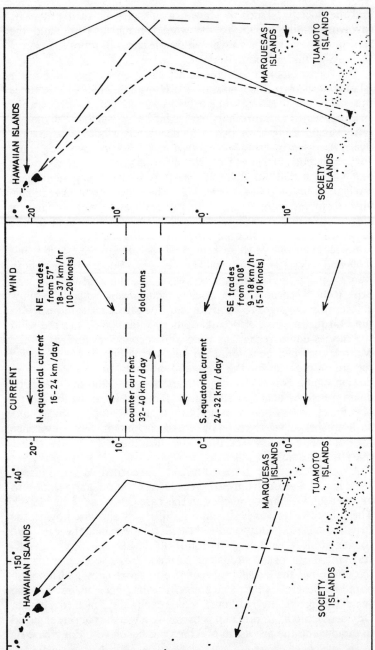

Fig. 19

speed noticeably. The problem was to find out if it is possible to row with oars placed in the position

$$2 \quad 1 \quad 2 \quad 1$$
$$1 \quad 2 \quad 1 \quad 2$$

At Portsmouth in 1970, a naval cutter designed for 12 men on 6 benches was adapted to allow 3 men to sit on each of the 4 after-benches, with extra rowlocks provided for the second oar in each alternate position (Fig. 20). Experiment showed that there was plenty of space beneath the arms and in front of the chest of the outboard man to allow the centre-line oar to be worked. The differences in leverage between outboard and centre-line oars was not great. Additionally, the siren vase shows a seventh oar-port, but only 6 oars; it is presumed that this extra oar-port would allow a division of the crew into 7 and 5 to counteract strong side winds, as in modern boats where 5 oars can be divided into $3+2$ or $2+3$ depending on wind and current. Odysseus' ship is likely, on the basis of this experiment, to have been both speedy and manoeuvrable, features of importance in any form of aggression.

Somewhat earlier in date are the vessels shown in the rock art of Scandinavia. These are of the Bronze Age and Iron Age, and some are of the second millennium B.C. The boats depicted in the engravings have been interpreted in various ways, as skin boats, planked boats, dugouts and rafts. Recent studies of some of the carvings from Ostfold in Norway have led to the assertion that these must represent skin-covered boats, with curved hulls and a double bow for beaching of the vessel (Fig. 21). In 1971 the BBC and the NRK (Norwegian State Broadcasting Organisation) financed the construction and testing of a boat based on this interpretation (Johnstone 1972). Alder and lime were used by an experienced ship-wright from Skeberg, and the wood was shaped

Fig. 19

Voyages in the Pacific (based on Finney 1967)
left: solid line, sailing from the Marquesas to Hawaii at 105° to the wind; long-dashed line, drifting before wind and current from the Marquesas; short-dashed line, sailing from the Society Islands to Hawaii at 95° to the wind
right: solid line, alternative route from Society Islands to Hawaii utilising countercurrent and doldrums, and sailed at 75° to the wind; long-dashed line, the voyage from Hawaii to the Marquesas involves sailing at 65° to the wind, experimentally impossible; short-dashed line, sailing from Hawaii to the Society and Tuamoto Islands at 75° to the wind

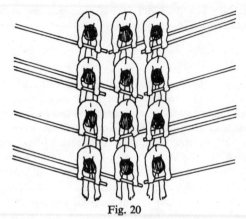

Fig. 20

Oarsmen in the ship of Odysseus (after Tilley 1971)

by axe, adze and knife; no saws were used and the only modern tool employed was a drill to make pegholes.

The kelson was 7 metres long and onto this was fitted stem and stern pieces, and 9 U-shaped frames, by wooden pegs. Chine members, gunwales and stringers were added, and the whole was then covered by 8 tanned cowhides stitched and glued together and laced onto the frame. A high inner bow and stern, thwarts and cross-pieces completed the vessel after the addition of a keel attached outside the skin. The boat was 7 metres long, 1·3 metres

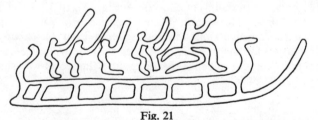

Fig. 21

Rock carving at Kalnes, Ostfold, Norway, the model for the reconstructed Bronze Age ship

wide and weighed 180 kg; it took the builder about 200 manhours to complete, plus the acquisition and treatment of the skins. A recent umiak of the same size occupied 3 men 3 weeks in its construction, plus the time needed to get 7 sealskins and stitch them together; so the two vessels were made in about the same time.

The Norwegian boat was then tested for seaworthiness and for load capacity. Its unladen freeboard was 50 cm, and with a crew of 6 and 600 kg of cargo this was only reduced to 32·5 cm; beyond this load the danger of swamping by waves was probably great. The boat could be paddled at 3 knots in easy conditions, unladen, and was very stable and dry. No rough weather was encountered but the double bow tended to cut small waves and lift the craft so that it rode easily. Beaching on pebble shores was simple, but it would have been useful to have had tests of rough weather for open-water suitability, and live animal cargo for strength of skins and frame. Nevertheless, the experiment shows the resemblance of skin boats to some of the rock engravings, and adds appreciably to our knowledge of the conditions under which early man may have peacefully colonised the islands in and around north-western Europe.

Many of the experiments involving long-distance travel have been undertaken in the Pacific Ocean where multiple island blocks and chains have allowed intercommunication and have provided landfalls within the enormous basin. The Easter Islands lie some 4000 km from South America, 3200 km beyond are the Tuamoto archipelago and the Society Islands leading eventually into Melanesia. In contrast, voyages across the mid-Atlantic Ocean are not provided with many such intermediate stages; it is over 4800 km of open water from the coast of north-west Africa to the West Indies, for the Azores to the north and the Cape Verde Islands to the south are not really practicable intermediate stops. The early voyages of Viking explorers and settlers tended naturally to utilise northern islands, Iceland, Greenland, Newfoundland, and their exploits are none the less impressive for it, but early journeys to central America would have involved far greater expanses of open uninterrupted water.

Several experiments have been carried out on Viking ships. Some of those which have survived were clearly for protected waters, being long and slender with a low freeboard and provision for a sail that might have been dangerous to raise in a strong breeze. Others are ocean-going vessels, broader and much deeper and a replica of one of these was sailed across the Atlantic in 1893 for the World's Fair in Chicago (Thorvildsen 1961, 26). In 1963 a replica of the Ladby ship from Denmark was made by a scout troop from Gram, Jutland (Crumlin–Pedersen 1969). Although this was not an exact copy, in that the strakes were of sawn boards, not adzed out, and were thicker, the experimental launchings and journeys showed that the original Ladby ship would have been

ideally suited for protected waters. It could be easily beached, and
drew little water so that it could be sailed or paddled up shallow
rivers. In 1967 a successful attempt was made to load 4 horses, to
sail with them, and to disembark them. The representations of
such operations in the Bayeux Tapestry are clearly accurate. More
recently, experimental work has been done on other Scandinavian
ships, including the Skuldelev long ship (Fig. 22) and a medieval
cargo ship from Frederikshaven. These have involved inshore
sailings, and few attempts have been made to test deep and open
water conditions. Not really within the compass of experimental
voyages in ancient craft are the various attempts to cross the
Atlantic following presumed Viking routes and the Vinland map,
from northern Europe to Iceland, Greenland and on to America
(e.g. Anderson 1967).

One expedition to test the potentialities of a mid-Atlantic
crossing was made in 1969 by Heyerdahl. The theory of an early

Fig. 22

Viking ship from Skuldelev, Denmark, reconstructed (after Crumlin-
Pedersen 1969)

discovery of the Americas by north African civilisations, principally Egyptian, is not at all proven, but the experiment was
designed to show if an Egyptian-type boat could have crossed the
Atlantic (Heyerdahl 1971).

Representations of ancient Egyptian boats which exist as wall
paintings and models in various tombs show that some were made
of reeds, bound together to form a double-pointed sailing vessel.
Similar boats are in use today in various areas of the world, and
Heyerdahl employed ship-wrights from Lake Tchad to make his
first reed boat called *Ra* (Pl. 9). This was 14 metres long, 4·5
metres wide, and was made entirely of papyrus reeds soaked in
water and bound together in bundles with rope. The vessel was
formed by 20 of these bundles, each running from bow to stern,
the total quantity of reeds estimated at 200 000. A small cabin,
$3 \times 3·5$ metres, was woven of reed and placed amidships. In front
of the cabin was an A-frame mast, and behind was a bridge carrying two long steering oars. The oars were of iroko wood, fixed
slantwise on the stern and joined together by a horizontal beam
on the bridge so that they moved in unison. The weight of the
craft was over 12 tons, plus a cargo of food and other equipment
and a crew of 7 men, a Norwegian, an American, a Russian, an
Italian, a Mexican, an Egyptian and a Moroccan.

The reed boat was made in Egypt and transported to Safi on the
Atlantic coast of Morocco. On 25 May it set sail and immediately
the two oars broke just above the wide blades; on the second day
the yard-arm cracked, thus foreshadowing a whole series of
similar accidents which plagued the voyage. Improvisation and
repair were features of the journey. However, the major problem
was not the steering oars or mast but the stern of the craft itself.
Egyptian representations showed a line from the upturned stern
running down to the after-deck, but this had been ignored in
building the *Ra*. The bow had a rope to the mast, and lines from
the mast ran back to the sides of the boat, the whole combining to
support the mast and to keep the bow up. The stern was not supported in this way, and it began to sag and brake the progress of
the boat.

After 25 days, over 1900 km had been achieved, and this was
followed by storms, another broken oar, the collapse of the
bridge, and the chopping up of the foam life-raft to help bolster
the stern; the foam pieces were soon washed away. The winds
were constantly blowing extra water onto starboard, and the reed
bundles here absorbed so much that a list to starboard developed
(Pl. 10). Forty days out, 3200 km sailed, the boat began to break

up as the ropes securing the outermost bundle to starboard chafed through. A further storm held up progress towards a rescue vessel, and prowling sharks prevented underwater repairs. Finally, after 56 days and 4300 km, the *Ra* was abandoned only 970 km from Barbados and the crew and cargo were taken on board a rescue vessel.

The lessons learned were soon utilised. Indians from Lake Titicaca were employed to make another reed boat, *Ra II*, in Morocco; this used 280000 reeds, and consisted of 2 rolls of papyrus with a third smaller roll squeezed between. The resulting boat was firm and did not undulate as had *Ra I*. The stern was tied down to the deck, and thick steering oars were made. The vessel was almost 12 metres long, and set sail for the New World from the same port. No problems were encountered at all except for a minor difficulty 4 days out when the boat began to sink; much cargo was quickly abandoned and the voyage continued. After 57 days, land was sighted, and the 5200 km from Morocco to Barbados were completed.

The experiment showed again that currents and winds were suitable for driving a craft across the Atlantic, and that a reed boat was capable of withstanding a long period of immersion in salt water and the heavy seas of the open ocean. It did not of course prove that ancient Egyptians did discover America, but only showed that it was possible for such early forms of craft to have made the journey. It would clearly be a case of one-way traffic, and not a series of voyages of discovery, report and colonisation.

Even without proof of such trans-Atlantic and trans-Pacific voyages, the bare evidence of early colonisation of most of the world's large land masses, and the limited results of experimental journeys and tests, show again the resourcefulness, ingenuity and determination of ancient men in surviving long sea passages, whether started accidentally or deliberately.

3

LIGHT INDUSTRY

The number of experiments concerned with reproducing and testing of small artifacts is considerable, both in the variety of materials and in the range of approaches. Copies of simple or complex objects have been made in attempts to emulate the technological processes employed in ancient times, and other copies have been made more rapidly, using modern equipment, the aim being to test the functional capabilities of the objects themselves. Some experiments have tried to do both.

The materials used for these purposes are described here under headings of stone, wood, bone and shell, metals, hides and textiles, and pottery; sections on the arts of painting and music in ancient times are also included. The scale of these experiments are as varied as the materials, and some have contributed considerably to our understanding of early technological processes and man's resourcefulness.

STONE-WORKING

Stone technology has been exploited in greater measure than any other aspect of experimental archaeology. Stone tools and their associated debris are far and away the most abundantly represented archaeological remains, rivalled only in later prehistoric times by potsherds. No doubt the earliest equipment of man consisted of stone, bone and wooden materials, but through the agencies of decay and erosion, only stones have survived from perhaps 99 per cent of all sites. Stone equipment therefore assumes an importance to studies of the earliest men beyond its contemporary value either then or now, since it represents the last chance to interpret and reconstruct certain ancient behaviour patterns.

The standardisation of stone tools over wide areas of land and periods of time suggests that they were tools for making other tools, of wood and bone, and their similarities are therefore functional and not cultural; this indicates that experimental work on their wear patterns may yield information of greater value than may a study merely of their production. Yet, for the very earliest times, and the earliest stone tools, the difficulties of recognition, the determination of human as opposed to natural character, is best approached through knowledge of technical processes obtained by experiment. Both lines, therefore, replication and function, can aid our understanding.

Many prehistorians are able to reproduce stone artifacts of the simplest types; pebble-tools, hand-axes and flake tools are easily made. Fewer are able to duplicate the production of blades, long parallel-sided flakes, generally punched off the core, and as few can replicate the more sophisticated shapes of the Old and New Stone Ages. The literature on this aspect of experimental work is vast, and a recent bibliography contains over 500 references (Hester 1972); collaboration between practitioners has been established through a new serial publication (Knudson and Muto). Only a few of these and other experiments can be described here.

The basic techniques that will succeed in breaking a large nodule of flint or other stone into manageable pieces have been demonstrated by Leakey, Coutier, Bordes and Barnes, among a host. The subsequent flaking of these pieces into recognisable shapes has again been well tested by continued experiment, using both stone hammers and bone or wooden hammers, and within 15 minutes a functional hand-axe can be produced. A recent experiment has carried this work a stage further by examining the waste flakes and chips produced during the shaping of a hand-axe (Newcomer 1971). Quartzite hammerstones and red deer antler hammers were used, and a number of hand-axes were produced. The first stage, involving the hammerstone roughing-out of a nodule of flint to an oval shape with cortex still remaining in places, produced 10 to 20 flakes characteristically thick. Next, the flint was thinned and shaped with heavy antler hammers, so that bumps and cortex were eliminated, and 10 or 20 thin flakes produced. Finally, the finishing of the hand-axe was done with a light antler hammer, producing 15 to 30 small thin flakes. The experimental method used allowed the nodule to be reconstituted by sticking together the 51 numbered flakes in one test; the very small chips of flint knocked off incidentally during the manufacture of this axe totalled an astonishing 4600. Such tiny chips should be present on prehistoric sites if axes had been made there, and excavators no doubt should look for them.

More sophisticated forms of flint equipment have also been replicated successfully by many archaeologists and others. The techniques employed include indirect percussion, with bone or antler punch, soft hammer percussion, and various forms of pressure-flaking. The production of bifacially-worked arrowheads, extremely thin and symmetrical, is often considered to have involved pressure-flaking of a highly developed and secret character, but recent experiments and observations have conceded that some types of controlled percussion can also replicate these shapes. The well-known Victorian craftsman Edward Simpson, more often called 'Flint Jack' among other less complimentary names, could reproduce many types of ancient implement, and often did so to enhance the collections of his wealthier contemporaries, but he could not reproduce the fine evenly-spaced flaking on some projectile heads of British, European or North American prehistoric date (Blacking 1953). Today a number of specialists can duplicate this finest form of stone retouch by a variety of skilfully controlled percussion and pressure.

The polishing of stone, such as was practised by many Neolithic communities of Europe, has also had its experimental practitioners. An early test suggests that a stone axe of moderate hardness could be flaked and then ground into shape in little over 4 hours' work (Evans 1897, 36), but some polished axes of particularly fine quality must have taken many more hours than this to achieve their sheen and beauty. The material used in grinding down a stone to a finished shape seems to have been sandstone containing quartz grains which is effective on many substances (Semenov 1964, 69). Although a chipped stone axe and a ground stone axe have been proved equally efficient in cutting down small trees (Leakey 1954, 141), experiments in general suggest that a smoothly shaped edge is slightly more efficient than an irregular flaked edge in chopping (but see p. 125).

The cutting or sawing of stone has always intrigued prehistorians who have sometimes found it difficult to visualise how a hard rock such as nephrite or diorite (greenstone) or various cherts could have been cut through without metal tools. Experiments with sharp flint flakes on a greenstone axe showed that some progress, laborious but inexorable, could be made in cutting through the stone in a sawing operation (Evans 1897, 45). A preferred method used on a steatite axe by Evans was with string and sand, the abrasive sand being put into operation by the sawing motion of the string. More recent work has shown that a wooden slat, or rush rope, or bone, or flint flake, when used with sand in this way can effectively cut through many rocks (Semenov 1964, 71). Water is generally required to keep the loosened dust washed away, as otherwise it will clog the sand action. Sandstone slabs, with narrowed edges, are also effective in sawing through other rocks.

The same basic procedure is employed in that other impressive feature of some Neolithic axes, the perforation for a handle (Pl. 3). Early experiments showed that it was possible to drill through a steatite axe with a flint flake, but a wooden stick twirling in a small pocket of sand on the stone was more successful (Evans 1897, 48). However, the success of this method should not disguise the laborious nature of the operation; in one experiment, an ash stick with sand abrasive managed to start a hole in diorite, and after 2 hours of drilling, the depression was 0·3 mm deep. Yet on catlinite, an ash drill and dry sand was highly successful in boring through the rock; pine wood was too soft, and water turned the rock dust into a sticky mess (Kidder, Jennings and Shook 1946, 122). Many authors have commented that the invention of the tubular drill saved much time and labour in reducing the amount of rock to be worn into dust; the saving is likely to be of the order of at least 50 per cent depending of course on the width of the flange on the tubular drill.

In the working of jade, tubular drills and abrasives have been observed to be effective (Smith and Kidder 1951, 39). The manufacture of Mayan jade ear-plugs involved very careful work with tubular drills of different sizes, solid drills of small diameter, and saws of narrow blade thickness. The product was finished by grinding and polishing (Fig. 23). Aztec ear-spools fashioned from obsidian have been replicated by drilling and turning with carefully prepared tools (Thomsen and Thomsen 1970). Ethnographic references do not describe the ancient processes, but the experiments were based upon the remarkable symmetry and uniformity of the ear-spools (Fig. 24a), which were clearly made with precision. Satisfactory copies were made by roughly shaping and drilling obsidian plugs, then rotating them on a mandrel or shaft driven by the 2-string floating method (Fig. 24b). Around the plug was held a 2-lap tube of metal and wood, with an abrasive powder, and pressure plus rotation resulted in the production of a smoothed blank for an ear-plug even when an eccentric perforation was provided

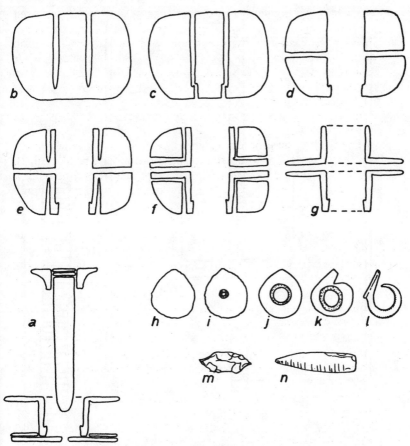

Fig. 23

a   Section through jade ear-plug assembly, Nebaj, Guatemala; upper
    rod with jade mosaic top enters jade flare with jade and slate
    backing discs (1/1)

b–g Manufacture of jade flare seen in section; *b* tubular drilled stone;
    c release of central core by further drilling; *d* horizontal saw to
    produce faces of flare pair; *e* tubular drilling of each piece;
    f removal of stone by sawing around the blanks to meet the drilled
    bases; *g* polished flares (after Smith and Kidder 1951)

h–n Manufacture of shell fishhook, California: *h* shell blank chipped
    to pear shape; *i* central hole drilled with chert drill (*m*); *j* hole en-
    larged and blank smoothed; *k* notch cut in; *l* ground and polished
    final product with shank and point; *m* chert drill; *n* stone file of
    basalt or sandstone. All about ½ (after Robinson 1942)

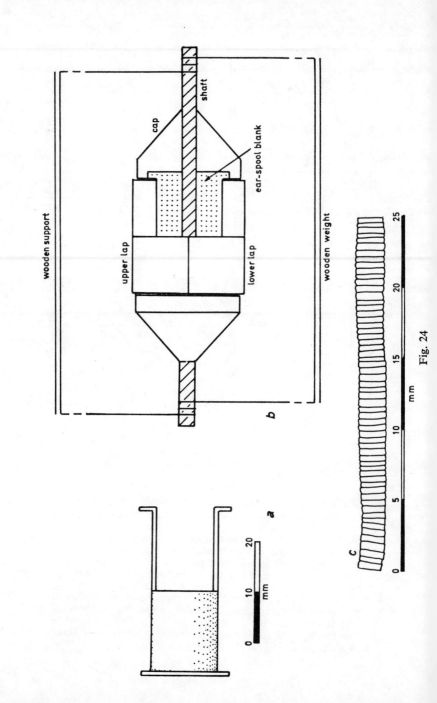

Fig. 24

on the plug; the method of rotation corrected this eccentricity by abrading unequally until concentricity was achieved.

The same processes were used in the production of nephrite Maori *hei tiki*, although some modern materials were used (Barrow 1962). A slab of nephrite was shaped by drilling (with a stick and abrasive powder), by shaving (with a stone flake), and by smoothing (with string and abrasive), into a small figure about 6 cm high. The time taken for this was 350 hours, and it seemed likely that an experienced Maori craftsman would have taken at least an appreciable portion of this time to produce such a small object to the normal high standard. The patience and perseverance required for the work was noted.

Similar qualities were essential in another experiment, that concerning the amazing bead necklaces found with burials in the cremation cemeteries of the Pueblo Indians in Arizona (Haury 1931). The beads are of stone, bone, shell or clay, and most are of a dark slate or argillitic rock available locally. The longest necklace recorded by Haury was 10 metres long, exhibited as 16 strands each 60 cm long. The beads, however, average 16 to each centimetre, making a total of over 15 000 in the admittedly enormously long necklace (Fig. 24,*c*). They average 2 mm in overall diameter, the size of an ordinary pin head, and the smallest from the area are 1·3 mm diameter; the thickness ranges from 0·25 mm to 1·0 mm. As small are the perforations, drilled neatly through at diameters of 0·5 to 1·0 mm. The finest sewing needle, no. 10, will just pass through the smallest perforation.

The drilling of stone beads was experimentally done using the most readily available sharp small and strong tool in the area, the spine of the cactus plants *Carnegiea gigantea* and *Echinocactus wislizeni*. A small stone plate was prepared by rubbing on an abrasive surface. A flint flake grooved this into segments 4 mm square, which were then broken off. A flint point made a small depression in the middle of the segment to provide a footing for the cactus drill. This was set into a notched stick and held with string; by rotating the stick between the hands, and pouring sand

Fig. 24

a Obsidian ear-spool showing section on the right

b Experimental method of producing ear-spool, side view on the left and section on the right. The shaped laps are held in place by a clasped hand as the shaft, cap and blank rotate (after Thomsen and Thomsen 1970)

c Stone beads from near Kayenta, Arizona. Note scale: about 60 beads to 25 mm (after Haury 1931)

and water into the hole, a perforation was made in 15 minutes. The hole was made uniform by turning it on the spine, and the segment was then rubbed into a circular form on sandstone. The faces were then ground smooth and the bead was complete and was exactly the same as the prehistoric examples. The method seems likely to have been used in prehistoric times, but no proof exists that it was done in precisely this way. In any case, the experiments allowed an estimate to be made of the amount of time needed to produce the necklace of 15000 beads. Allowing only 15 minutes per bead, including gathering of material, cutting and breaking, drilling, rolling and polishing, the necklace would take 480 man-days at 8 hours per day, a notable task for a perfectionist craftsman.

Larger-sized stone beads would not involve quite as much effort in handling and finishing, but even with rather elaborate equipment, the production of beads for personal decoration is a skilled operation in many societies (e.g. Shaw 1945).

These experiments and many others have been concerned with the manufacture of stone equipment. The other aspect, the study of the functional capabilities of such equipment, has been far less extensively examined, yet in many ways this could be of greater value to archaeology. The basic shapes of stone tools—axes, knives, awls, scrapers and the like—remained unchanged over many centuries and in some cases millennia, and this must reflect common functions in part at least concerned with the shaping of tools of bone, antler and wood. Only by studies of wear patterns on surviving stone tools may we be able to gauge the importance of such organic materials. In addition, to take one example, stone 'celts' have been described in the past as axes, adzes, hoes, chisels, wedges, spades, picks and so on, and their use has been considered in terms of fighting, digging, chopping, butchering, mining, polishing, ceremonial practices, etc. Yet basically the 'celt' is a standardised shape, and the only ways by which some suggested use can be demonstrated are association and wear. It seems necessary to avoid the common circular argument that is present in much classification of ancient material; if an object looks as if it might have worked as a particular tool, let us say a hoe, it will be described as such. It then may become the standard by which other objects also are described as hoes, and a class of hoes is built up on a presumption that is not founded on anything but a vague resemblance and a subjective notion. Hence the value of wear patterns on ancient material.

The work of Semenov in Russia has concentrated on traces of wear upon stone equipment from the Upper Palaeolithic and later periods (1964). The scratches and striations on flints have been interpreted by microscopic study, and by comparison with experimentally reproduced marks, to represent certain ways in which the tools were held, the direction in which they were moved, and the material upon which they were active (Fig. 25). The point

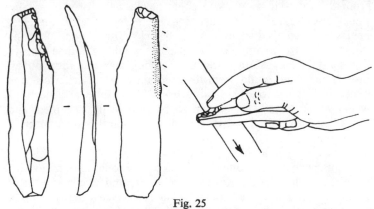

Fig. 25

Use of flint blade as whittling knife; stipple shows area of wear-marks, and lines show their direction (after Semenov 1964)

has been made that flint when freshly struck is so sharp and effective that it will cut or scratch almost any other stone, as well as bone, antler, horn and wood, and some metals, and so traces of wear upon flint are vital in determining any previous use; its potential is very great and almost unlimited in terms of the materials available to ancient man. Among the many deductions produced by this work, the conclusions that Upper Palaeolithic 'end scrapers' must have been used in particular ways in the flensing of skins, that long flakes probably were whittling knives and meat knives, and that not all 'burins' actually served as engraving tools, have opened up new areas of interest to prehistorians concerned with the functional potential of these industries of 20 000 years ago.

Another example of the value of wear studies on ancient materials concerns stone 'celts' as noted above (Sonnenfeld 1963). The interpretation of wear on a selection of chipped and ground celts from Delaware was deduced by comparisons with artifacts of known recorded function, and by experimental testing to produce comparable wear. In the event, much attention was directed towards the tool known as the stone hoe, in the belief that the traces of wear on a hoe should be easily distinguishable from those on a wood-chopping celt, or a celt used to bash skulls.

A series of hoes was collected, and various hafts were devised for these; the hoes were of slate, fine-grained silicates and quartzites and were either unused or resharpened. About 10 hoes were tested on soils of one sort or another, and in all cases the wear on the blade was clearly defined. Softer stone was smoothed and eroded, harder stone was scratched; bevels were formed by continued use, and a soil encrustation was noted on all blades just behind the damaged scoured area. The cleaning of possible stone hoes by their discoverers or in museums would of course remove this tell-tale encrustation. Scour-grooving was recorded on all hoes tested, and would seem to represent a useful criterion, one which in fact led to a re-classification of celts in local collections where some 'hoes' were shown to be incorrectly identified, and some 'axes' as well. The question of agricultural hoe as opposed to digging tool could not be answered of course, but the results seem extremely valuable.

A final experiment on edge-damage of stone equipment was concerned with the development of wear, and resulting loss of efficiency, on a variety of tools (Keller 1966). Wear depends upon 4 factors, the material of the tool, the shape of its edge, its manner of use, and the material upon which it was employed; in the experiments, the manner of use was tested, and the other factors were held more or less constant.

Tools were made of obsidian, and were used on manzanita wood (*Arctostaphylos* sp.) as well as on softer pine (*Pinus pardyana*) and on cow-hide. The operations performed included chopping, cutting and scraping, and the individual actions were repeated from 400 to 2400 times in each experiment. Records were made of the number of times (strokes) each tool was used before it ceased to be effective in whatever operation it was performing, and the point at which edge-stability was reached was also noted.

	Operation	Material	End of efficiency of tool	Edge- stability of tool	Total strokes delivered
1.	Chop	hardwood	200	650	1550
2.	Chop	hardwood	250	450	850
3.	Cut	hardwood	50	270	420
4.	Pare	hardwood	60	240	600
5.	Pare	softwood	735	750	810
6.	Saw	hardwood	600	600	1000
7.	Scrape	hardwood	>2470	470	2470
8.	Scrape	cow-hide	90	500	1600

The table points out that softwood and hardwood react differently to stone tools; the cutting edge in operation 4 was dull after only 60 strokes, but on softwood it was effective for 12 times as long. The damage to the tools, chipping and then smoothing, continued unequally beyond these points with little effect on the wood. In operation 7, the scraping edge of the tool was soon stabilised but it continued to be effective so long as the operation was continued. The type of damage to the various tools was also recorded for comparison with ancient artifacts, and some idea of the efficiency of different actions could be noted too; thus, scraping is more efficient than paring (operations 4 and 7), as the scraping tool would not need to be resharpened. The relative amount of time spent on certain activities on ancient occupation sites can be deduced by this type of investigation; equal numbers of cutting and scraping tools, for instance, should mean more time spent in scraping activities than in cutting as scrapers last much longer.

Work along these lines, the function and efficiency of stone tools, deduced through wear patterns and experiments, is one of the most promising approaches to stone studies that exist today.

WOOD-WORKING AND WEAPONS

Experimental work concerned with wood has been fairly restricted; the rarity of wooden remains in archaeological contexts may have contributed to this. Wood has often been used in the testing of other materials or methods, tree-felling by stone axes (p. 20), house-building (p. 57), or boat-building (p. 106), and there have been some references to the ease by which simple wooden equipment could be made. Spears and clubs were made using only unretouched flint flakes (Leakey 1954, 141), and some comparisons have been drawn between the ease of working wood by stone and steel chisels (McEwen 1946); in carving a *wheku* type of Maori head, the efficiency of the local greenstone chisel, with its rounded sides, was demonstrated, but the vital point made was that it was almost impossible to distinguish between the marks made by stone tools or 'primitive' steel tools on the wood itself.

A recent experiment was devised to test the ease with which certain wooden objects could be made by using stone tools (Crabtree and Davis 1968). Pegs for stretching hides, and paddles for pottery moulding, were experimentally made, using hard black oak for the paddles, and softer fresh willow for the pegs (Fig. 26); fire was employed in addition to the stone tools in one test. The work was improvised, stone tools made and procedures devised

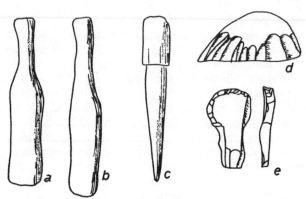

Fig. 26

a, b Oakwood paddles for pottery-making, shaped (*a*) without and
(*b*) with fire (1/5)
c Willow peg for stretching hides (3/5)
d, e Stone chopper and end-scraper (1/4)
(after Crabtree and Davis 1968)

as required. A peg was made by slicing a willow branch from a
tree, cutting it into shape, removing its bark, whittling and fire-
hardening a point, all done with obsidian flakes and taking but
30 minutes.

In working with the harder wood, an antler wedge, a heavy
high-backed plane and a scraper were also needed. One paddle
was made in 2½ hours by adzing, splitting, planing and grinding a
piece of oak (*Quercus kelloggii*). Another was made by chopping
or adzing the wood, then alternately burning and quenching, and
continually scraping off the charcoal. The paddle was finished off
by scraping, and took under 2 hours. Many observations were
made on the stone tools used and their edge-damage, and one
important point was that the working of hard woods, and to some
extent soft woods, involves many stone tools that are rapidly
exhausted in use (see p. 121).

The use of fire to shape wood is well-known, and dugout canoes
in many areas are made by fire-setting, adzing and scraping in
series. The belief that fire can harden wood, such as a spear point,
has been tested and shown to be erroneous, and it seems likely
that the shaping of wood is the principal use of fire in this respect
(Cosner 1956). Pairs of hardwood and softwood points were
made, one of each pair by shaving and grinding, the other by
charring. After repeated thrusts into an abrasive soil, no differences
in the two sets were apparent and the conclusion was that fire-

hardening as a phenomenon was unjustifiable. This experiment requires further examination and duplication to confirm the result.

Another use for fire, of course, is light, and experiments on torches have been made at Salts Cave, Kentucky (Watson 1969, 33). The remains of many weed stalks (*Gerardia* or *Solidago*) and canes (*Arundinaria*), bound by bark strips or grass, have been recovered from the site, and these allowed reconstructions to be made using the same materials growing locally. The most efficient torches were about 1 metre long, containing three 1–2 cm diameter canes; ragweed torches burned nearly twice as fast as a cane torch and produced much more smoke. A cane torch would last perhaps 45 minutes, and in using these within the cave, it was found that charcoal smudges resembling ancient marks would be deposited on cave walls and low ceilings where the ash was knocked off the torch end, that smoke from even cane torches caused eye and nose irritation, and that hot embers falling to the ground were a real hazard to any barefoot cave explorer.

In addition to the experiments noted above, which have been primarily concerned with the basic working of wood, another group has been directed towards the functional testing of finished products. In these, the most detailed work has been done on weapons of various sorts, mostly propelling arrows, and the equipment studied included bows, arrowshafts, spear-throwers and Roman artillery.

Perhaps the most ambitious attempt yet made to study the capabilities of the bow and arrow is the work done by Pope (1918). His experiments tested the shooting qualities of a wide range of bows, and the penetration of arrows. The bows selected for testing came from a wide range of sources, and each was examined for its cast (the capacity of a bow to throw an arrow) and its weight (the force needed to draw the bow string 71 cm from the back of the bow, measured by springs or weights). Several hundred arrows were also tested.

The average archer cannot draw a bow more than 73 cm which is about the distance from the extended left arm to the flexed right arm, and most of the Indian bows tested required an average draw of 65 cm. In the shooting experiments, both the Sioux and the English release were used; in the Sioux, all the fingers and the thumb are on the string, the nock of the arrow held by thumb and finger 1, while in the English, fingers 1–3 draw the string and the arrow is held between fingers 1 and 2, the thumb not being used.

The bows tested included Apache hickory, Cheyenne ash, African ironwood, Tartar and Turkish composites (horn, metal, wood, sinew), and English yew long-bows. Experiments on yew wood showed that fine-grained reddish wood was stronger than whitish sapwood; the latter however was extremely elastic and could be bent double without breaking. Bowstrings of linen thread, silk thread, catgut and cotton thread were tested to breaking, and the strongest proved to be Irish 60-strand linen thread, 3 mm diameter.

Some of the results of the experimental shooting of these bows appear in the table:

Type	Material	Length m	Drawn m	Weight kg	Range m
1. Apache	hickory	1·04	0·56	12·7	110
2. Cheyenne	ash	1·14	0·51	30·5	150
3. Cheyenne	ash		0·61	36·5	
4. Tartar	composite	1·88	0·71	13·7	91
5. Tartar	composite		0·91		102
6. Tartar	composite	1·88	0·74	c. 45·0	82
7. Tartar	composite		0·91		100
8. Polynesian	hardwood	2·00	0·71	22	149
9. Turkish	composite	1·22	0·74	38·5	229, 243, 257
10. English	yew	2·00	0·71	24·7	169
11. English	yew		0·91	32·7	107, 194
12. English	yew	1·83	0·91	28·1	208
13. English	yew	1·73	0·71	31·7	224

In test 6, the bow used was extremely large, with a bowstring of rawhide rope, and it was necessary to clamp it and employ 2 men to brace and string it. It could not be drawn by one man more than 30 cm, so it was shot by the archer lying on his back and bracing his feet against the bow, drawing it with both hands. Its performance was poor, but the bow was about one century old; its original owner was reported to have been able to string it and shoot it singlehanded, and shoot an arrow 400 metres. The bow in test 9 was made for the experiment, of cow-horn strips, hickory wood, catgut and raw hide (Pl. 11*a*,*b*); the varying distances were achieved with different arrows, the farthest with a bamboo arrow tipped with a rifle bullet jacket. A replica English long-bow for tests 10–13 was made of yew (Pl. 11*c*,*d*); its draw weight was low compared with other bows, and in test 11 the bamboo arrow travelled much farther than an English broad-head arrow. The reduction in length of this bow resulted in greater distance. In England, a reconstruction of a Neolithic yew long-bow at Cambridge was successful in shooting an arrow 60 metres; the bow was 190 cm long, and the original, the first English long-bow, dates to 2800 B.C. (Clark 1963).

The arrows tested by Pope included Californian Indian bamboo arrows with birch foreshafts, and tipped with low-cropped turkey feathers; these were 63 and 74 cm long, and carried about 10 per cent farther than English arrows and 20 per cent farther than normal target arrows. They were used for all the bows tested, but a large variety were tested in terms of woods, feathering, lengths and heads. Hickory, birch, ash, pine and willow were ranged in that descending order in terms of rigidity, with the first two much in advance of the others. It has been shown that heated grooved stones are very effective in straightening reed cane (*Phragmites communis*) arrow-shafts, but not solid wood shafts which can be heated and straightened by hand (Cosner 1951).

In the experimental shooting, average arrow velocities of 36 m per second were reached; this is 130 kph or 80 mph. Earlier tests in England had shown that a pinewood arrow tipped with a steel point and shot from a 29·5 kg bow at 7 metres penetrated 140 sheets of field-gun penetration pads, compared with the 35 sheets penetrated by a 14-gauge shot-gun. Even earlier records tell of Spanish explorers in Florida offering a native his freedom if he could shoot through a coat of mail at 150 paces; this he did, through 2 suits of chain mail, with a flint-tipped reed arrow, and this persuaded the Spanish to abandon chain mail and adopt felt cloth padding instead.

The arrowheads used in Pope's experiments included blunt-ended wood and metal, conical metal points, obsidian points, steel blades and bodkins, and barbed points (Pl. 12). These were shot uniformly at 22 mm thick green pinewood planks, and into simulated animal bodies consisting of open-sided boxes filled with animal livers and covered with deer hide. The blunt-ended arrows bounced off the yielding body, but would penetrate small animals whose bones would resist and therefore break. The obsidian point drove through the box, and several of the heavier metal arrow-blades also penetrated well into the box or completely through. None, however, were as effective as the obsidian, the wavy edge of which cut more readily than any smooth metal edge. One further test was made in emulation of the Florida native. A suit of sixteenth-century chain mail from Damascus was dressed onto a dummy body and shot at with a 34 kg bow, armed with a steel bodkin arrow, from 75 metres. The arrow struck the armour with a shower of sparks and went through it, through the 20 cm of simulated human behind the armour, and came to rest against the back of the chain mail. In the light of this, 'the experiment of shooting a broadhead [metal arrowhead] at this valuable musem specimen did not seem justified' (Pope 1918, 370). Recent

reconstructions of Roman scale armour have also not extended
to testing their resistance to attack (Robinson 1972).

Final tests of the penetration and killing power of arrows were
carried out in the field. A running buck deer was killed with a single
arrow, shot from 75 metres, that entered the chest and drove out
on the opposite side. Eight deer were killed in this way, as well as
3 adult bears and 2 cubs. Two adults were killed by arrows in the
chest and heart at 60 and 40 metres. A charging female, shot while
her cubs were being taken, received and resisted 5 arrows, one of
which passed through her abdomen and flew out 10 metres,
another of which buried itself in her chest; she was finally stopped
by a rifle shot that broke her foreleg. The experimenters' comment,
'These bears were wild and taken at great risk', does not seem to
be an exaggeration. Some comparisons were made between the
stopping power of arrows and bullets; the tearing of tissue by a
bullet is far greater than that by an arrow, but the cleaner cut of
an arrow allows more rapid loss of blood and may kill sooner.
The clean cut also allows an escaped animal to recover more
readily. 'So on the whole we feel that the bow is a more humane
and more sportsmanlike implement for hunting' (Pope 1918, 373).
Whether or not the victims felt the same way is debatable (Fig. 27).

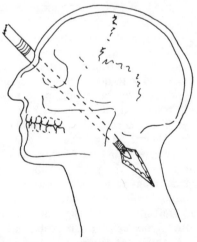

Fig. 27

Sketch of skull found near Buena Vista, California, with wooden
arrowshaft driven through right eye and out behind left part of jaw;
arrowhead of stone restored on basis of damage to bones. Death
rapid due to haemorrhage (after Pope 1918)

The same comment about projectile points has been made by other hunters, that their main purpose is to pierce the hide and enter the body at sufficient depth to cause haemorrhage and death. The optimum size of point obviously varies but a range between 3 and 5 cm seems generally acceptable; there is some argument about the claim that larger points, up to 12 cm long and weighing 90 grams, increases accuracy (Evans 1957).

In a small series of experiments, tests for accuracy and penetration of arrows shot from a bow and propelled from an atlatl (spear-thrower) were compared (Browne 1940). Wooden atlatls to replicate American Basket Maker implements, and a bow of 27 kg weight, were made and tests of accuracy were based on continued practice and experiment. It was found that the accuracy of the atlatl and its spear was very poor; the increased effective length of the arm in using the atlatl caused an irregular and uncontrolled thrust, and in the tests only 6 out of 36 spears hit an archery target at 30 metres. In contrast, an arrow shot from a bow by the same marksman hit the target 31 out of 36 times. The use of weights on atlatls helps increase balance but not velocity (Peets 1960). The conclusion was that hunters with atlatls and spears probably operated from ambush or close range, and shot into herds of animals. At 30 metres, spears and arrows penetrated wooden planks equally well, when tipped with a steel point. Browne also used this point on an arrow shot through an elk in Wyoming. The comment has also been made that the atlatl would have been eminently suitable for use in hurling harpoons, and that the discovery of many weights for atlatls along river courses is to be expected; experiments in propelling harpoons at fish with the bow, as opposed to the atlatl, proved to be 'spectacular failures' although the archer was very experienced (Peets 1960).

Other tests with atlatls have indicated a maximum range of 100 metres, with accuracy and penetration possible up to about 40 metres (Hill 1948). The efficiency of the atlatl for short-range shooting is attested by its wide popularity in America (Kellar 1955), and by observations on the extreme accuracy with which Bering Strait Eskimos could kill both seals and waterfowl at 30 metres or more (Nelson 1899, 152).

Of those who have tested bows and spear-throwers, almost all have argued that the arrow or spear, armed with a stone or metal point, is a highly efficient weapon, well able to penetrate animals at appreciable ranges of 50–100 metres. Any increase in range was probably not required until more organised forms of human conflict, involving defensive fortifications, had developed; in

Europe, various types of artillery were invented and used to great effect by the Romans in their conquest of northern lands. Records exist of some of these pieces of equipment, and a few experiments have been made in reconstructing and testing forms of Roman ballista (Marsden 1971).

At Maiden Castle, Dorset, the multiplication of the defensive earthworks suggested that a need was felt to keep attackers at long range, and the discovery within the fortress of dumps of sling stones indicated the nature of certain projectiles. The elevated rampart walks would of course have given an advantage to the defenders. Slings probably had a range of 100 metres, but their accuracy and force at this distance is likely to have been slight. The capture of Maiden Castle by a Roman army in A.D. 44 may have been the result of superior forces and organisation, but the discovery of an iron projectile head in a human vertebra in the fort's war cemetery suggested that Roman siege artillery had been employed to fire heavy arrows from outside the range of sling stones into the fortress. A replica of a Roman ballista was used to demonstrate the power of this armament (Johnstone 1957).

The Roman ballista (Pl. 15) existed in many different calibres, depending on the weight of shot it was to propel. The standard formula was based on the diameter of the spring required to fire the given weight a standard distance of 400–500 metres:

$$D = 1 \cdot 1 \times \sqrt[3]{100M}$$

where D is the diameter of the spring in dactyls (1 dactyl = 19 mm) and M is the weight of shot in minae (1 mina = 440 g). All of the parts of the ballista depended on D, as they all were multiples of D, and all the calibres were geometrically identical. The ballista consisted of a string attached to 2 wooden arms bedded in twisted gut skeins (the springs); the string was hauled back by ratchet lever and it was attached to a propelling plate sliding in a trough, in which the arrow lay. Various replicas of this model have been made, sometimes using modern materials, as exercises in engineering principles, and in tests they have shown the power generated by the springs and the force of the arrow as it leaves the machine. Clearly the possession of artillery such as this gave the Romans an advantage over their enemies equal to the rifle over the bow and arrow.

WORKING IN BONE, ANTLER AND SHELL

One of the most readily available sources of material for tools is bone, antler, ivory and horn, obtainable from the remains of food animals, and there now seems little doubt that this material was used from very early times. Worked bones have been recovered from some east African sites that may be upwards of a million years old, and the well-known Osteodontokeratic industries from the Transvaal, if truly of hominid character, show the quite explicit use of bone, tooth and horn in the Early to Middle Pleistocene; this material is, however, still not universally acknowledged to have been deliberately shaped.

Much importance therefore attaches to experimental studies on crushing and breaking of bone for marrow extraction by man, and to observations of animal action, and natural erosion, that also alter bone. Some of this work has demonstrated that functional shapes, points in particular, occur normally if a bone is smashed by random blows (Harrisson and Medway 1962), and gnawing by carnivores, rodents and porcupines can produce wear marks that may mislead the archaeologist.

The Middle Pleistocene kill-sites at Torralba and Ambrona, Spain, contain many remains of elephant (*Palaeoloxodon antiquus*), the bones of which were split and smashed for marrow extraction, but in this case experiment has shown that some of the bone pieces must have been flaked and trimmed in a deliberate manner to produce functional implements; the rarity of suitable stone for tools in the area probably encouraged the hunters to use bone (Biberson and Aguirre 1965).

Bones and teeth are easily altered, and Charles Dawson, of Piltdown fame, experimentally stained bones as well as flints to see if they resembled material said to be from the site. Later investigators of the Piltdown problem showed that by filing and staining a chimpanzee molar, it came to resemble a Piltdown molar; the elephant femur club from the site was also shown experimentally to have been shaped by a metal blade (Weiner 1955). In somewhat similar fashion, experimental work has shown that a human body, considered to have been ritually chopped up by Neolithic occupants of Maiden Castle, Dorset, had suffered wounds not from a stone but from a metal blade (Brothwell 1971). This particular Neolithic ritual practice is therefore discounted, and a radiocarbon date has helpfully indicated a post-Roman date for the body and its wounds.

These experiments have shown how easy it is to break and flake bone, and how other features must be used in attempts to decide if human selection and action were involved in bone tool manufacture. Although great quantities of recognisable bone equipment exist, from at least 30000 years ago, few experiments have been carried out on their production. Early Neolithic bone spoons, from selected areas of south-eastern Europe, have been shown to represent a standardised method of manufacture, involving the splitting of a *Bos primigenius* metacarpal bone, its fracture by grooving and snapping, then grinding it into shape (Nandris 1971).

Of equal interest to those experiments concerned with the processing of bone are those involved with understanding the uses to which specific bone tools were put. Many bone implements—awls, needles, harpoons, and so on—seem obvious in their function, but others require more consideration and in some cases experiment. One of the latter was concerned with the interpretation of notched ribs and scapulae of large game animals hunted by Basket Maker Indians from Colorado (Morris and Burgh 1954, 60).

The suggestion that these tools were used in beaming operations on hides was disproved by scraping a green deer hide with both unnotched and notched ribs; the former was more effective, and the prongs of the latter broke off. A major industry of the society was the production of cordage, using the leaves of the yucca plant (*Yucca* sp.). Local yucca leaves were collected, up to 50cm in length and 1cm in width; a tough bark-like covering encloses light-coloured parallel longitudinal fibres within the leaf. The edges of the leaf were stripped off, then the leaf was drawn over a pole and hammered with a stone until the bark was smashed and the fibres beaten apart. A smooth rib bone scraped much of the pulp from the leaf, and the fibres from several leaves were collected, washed and scraped with smooth and notched ribs. The notched rib was very effective, working like a comb, clearing out bits of pulp, and eventually a clean white hank of fibre was produced ready for twisting into cord. A notched rib from a site in the area contained a smear of fibres and dried sap from the yucca plant, and more or less confirmed the experimentally derived idea that notched ribs were scraping combs for preparation of fibre. Ethnographic evidence from the area also supported this interpretation, although many other groups used only fingers and teeth to separate pulp from fibre.

Fresh bone of large mammals is particularly suitable for tools that are to be applied to resistant materials, and the age of the animal is sometimes also important to consider. In Denmark, a

hoard of Neolithic bone and flint chisels was recovered, and provided models for reconstruction made from cow metatarsal bones
(Becker 1962). Elderly cows were selected so that the bone would
be firm and hard. On dry seasoned wood, the chisels worked
poorly, splintering the wood and chisels alike, but on green alder,
using a wooden mallet, it was possible to cut rectangular holes
through 5 cm diameter stems (Fig. 28). The shaping of a mortice

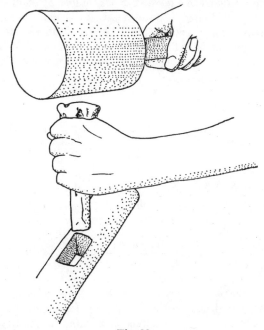

Fig. 28

Sketch to show method of cutting mortices in soft wood by bone
chisel and mallet (after Becker 1962)

and tenon joint was accomplished in 1 hour, with little resharpening of the chisel needed. The chisels were not considered to be
fine enough for delicate work, decorative carving for example, but
were admirably suited for rougher carpentry. In this case, it
would have been interesting to work with a greater variety of
woods, and with younger bone. Rather similar implements, of
moose metatarsus or bear ulna, were recently used to deflesh hides
in Canada (Steinbring 1966).

   In addition to bone, antler was a popular material for the production of equipment, particularly among hunting groups basing

their economy upon deer and reindeer. One of the features of the late glacial and early post-glacial societies of southern France and northern Spain, 12000–7000 B.C., was their interest in hunting with harpoons. We do not know what animals were killed with these, and no spear-throwers have survived from this period although earlier ones are known. The harpoon heads are generally small, 12 cm long, but no bows are known and the problems of harpoon-shooting from a bow have been noted by several authors.

In a study of these harpoon-heads, an attempt was made to discover why their shapes differed between the various regions. In France, the heads had bulbs at the base and were biserially-barbed (Fig. 29*a,b*), in northern Spain contemporary heads had

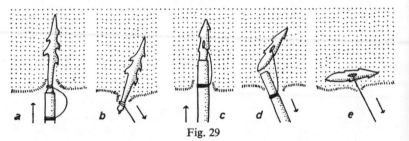

Fig. 29

Harpoons (after Thompson 1954). Arrows show direction of thrust or drag
a, b Magdalenian harpoon likely to pull out when shaft caught
c–e Azilian harpoon tends to swivel and block withdrawal when shaft caught

asymmetrically-placed perforations and were uniserially-barbed. Later, post-glacial, harpoon-heads in Spain had a central perforation (Fig. 29*c–e*). Reconstructions were made of these types, they were hurled at pillows stuffed with hair, and then the line attaching them to the shaft was tugged (Thompson 1954). The bulb-ended harpoon tended to pull out, the earlier Spanish harpoon tended to swivel sideways, and the centrally-perforated harpoon turned sideways and came to rest inside the pillow. The conjectured reason for these shapes was that in late-glacial France, tundra conditions would have existed, and a shaft would have dragged readily along the ground, gradually slowing the wounded animal. In Spain, however, such conditions would not have existed, and the denser brushwood would have caught and held the shaft; the animal would therefore either have been captured, or it would have pulled out the harpoon-head in its struggles. The invention of a toggle-effect harpoon was a necessity.

A similar effect was achieved for the same reason in the manufacture of shell fish-hooks by the Chumash Indians of southern California. These fishermen, recorded by Spanish explorers in the eighteenth century, were successful exploiters of coastal waters, catching tunny, sea bass, barbel and sardine from canoes with milkweed fibre lines, stone sinkers and shell hooks. The hooks were made of abalone (*Haliotis*) and mussel (*Mytilus*) shell, and were from 10 to 60cm long. They were deeply incurved and most had a grooved shank in which the line was lashed.

In experimental work on these hooks, various replicas were made, by chipping, drilling and grinding (Fig. 23*h–n*); the tools used, duplicating those found in the middens of the Chumash, included chert drills and stone files, and the time taken to produce a hook was from 1·5 to 2·5 hours (Robinson 1942). In tests with these hooks, numerous fish, mostly bottom-feeding rockfish, bass and halibut, were caught, and every fish had worked the thin tissues at the side of its mouth through the clearance between the point and the shank of the hook when the steady pull of the line rotated the hook and caused the point to slide through. Escape with this hook, versions of which are widely used throughout the Pacific, was judged to be almost impossible. The contrast with the European barbed hook is that the latter is struck to fix the barb in the mouth, while the former is never struck when the fish bites, but merely gently tensioned to allow the pull of the line from the inner shank head to rotate the hook and set it more and more firmly in the jaw.

There is no doubt that experiments carried out under as normal conditions as possible are more valuable than those that take place under artificial circumstances. The testing of projectiles, for example, is more telling and dramatic when conducted against likely victims, deer or bear, than against pillows or boxes, and no amount of theoretical statement on the value of shanked shell fish-hooks can match the demonstrable evidence of their practical nature in catching and holding fish. Some experiments, however, cannot be conducted on their natural materials or under their natural circumstances, and among these are tests on live human bodies. Two experiments concerned with the treatment of human material are those of trephining and mummification.

From many areas of the world, skulls exist that have had roundels of bone removed by cutting and levering (Pl. 13). Among certain recent societies, this act has the effect of relieving the living person of his particular illness or obsession, perhaps by providing him with alternative problems. In the nineteenth century, however, the discovery in tombs of trephined skulls led to the theory that the operation must have been conducted posthumously. Experiments were conducted on an adult skull and a child's skull, using glass flakes, and while the child's skull was relieved of its roundel in only 4 minutes, the thicker adult skull resisted for 50 minutes (Munro 1897, 220). The conclusion was that only a child could have survived the operation, as no adult could withstand almost an hour of scraping. More recent discoveries and observations have shown that an adult can indeed survive the ordeal, that it can be done in less than 30 minutes, and that certain adults were subjected for whatever reason to repeated roundel-removals, and survived for at least a time. The record seems to be 7 discs removed before the peace of death ensued, by which time the individual had little covering his brain.

Experiments on mummification have not been carried out, so far as is known, on recent humans, although the drying of bodies and removal of internal parts is practised in various societies around the world. The archaeological problem, however, concerned the claim that bodies in ancient Egypt were soaked and softened before packing (Lucas 1962). Experiments were conducted on chickens, and three of these, plucked and eviscerated, were soaked for 70 days in an 8 per cent solution of natron or similar solution of salt. All were very soft and partly damaged after this soaking, and it seemed an unlikely method in the mummification process, but they were dried and kept successfully in this state for 13 years before being disposed of. Further experiments were done on pigeons, to test if the damage done by soaking of bodies in natron or salt could be avoided by using dry natron and salt. A 3 per cent solution of both natron and salt was used this time in the soaking tests; for the dry tests, the bodies were buried in pottery vessels and surrounded by natron or salt. All 4 tests, dry salt, dry natron, wet salt, wet natron, were carried out for 40 days. The body from the salt solution was very badly disintegrated, that from the natron solution was plump and in good condition, but smelled of putrefaction for several weeks after drying. The bodies from the dry natron and salt were hard, emaciated and dry; no putrefaction smell was noted.

The results of the experiments were that birds might be preserved by soaking in 8 per cent natron for 70 days, or 3 per cent natron for 40 days, or by packing them in dry natron or salt for 40 days. The theoretical conclusion was that the essential operation of mummification in Egypt was the dessication of the body, and therefore that deliberate drying of the body was the major feature and was caused by burial in dry natron and not in a solution. These conclusions seem to be supported by archaeological evidence, but the experiments as such could not claim to be entirely definitive.

WORKING WITH METALS

There have been many experiments concerned with the metals most commonly used by prehistoric man, copper and bronze, gold and iron. The production of objects from these metals involved not only the shaping, by casting or forging, of the metals but also the collection and treatment by smelting of the various ores. Experiments have been carried out on many of these processes.

The simplest of the copper ores to smelt are oxides from weathered surfaces of copper-bearing deposits. At 700–800°C carbonate ores can be reduced to copper metal, and one experiment attempted to smelt these ores in a small pit in the ground without a draught (Coghlan 1940). A pit was dug and dried out by fire, then a circle of stone slabs was placed around the pit, forming an enclosure 1 metre across. A charcoal fire was lit, and a cone of charcoal was piled up with the malachite ore buried in its centre. After several hours of intense heat, the malachite (and cuprite in a subsequent experiment) had been converted to a black copper oxide, and no metal had been produced. The temperature of an open fire is 600–700°C, and the ores could easily have been converted to black oxides in this; the reason for the failure of the test was apparently the excess of air in the pit. A further experiment, with malachite placed beneath an inverted pottery vessel, the whole buried and heated as before, yielded a spongy metallic copper, and finally a small bead of metal was produced when finely-ground malachite was heated in the same way.

An experiment in Cambridge carried out a few years ago on oxides, with forced air draught in a pit, achieved 1100°C and reduced the oxide to metallic copper:

$$CuO \quad + \quad CO \quad \rightarrow \quad Cu \quad + \quad CO_2$$

CuO	+	CO	→	Cu	+	CO$_2$
(copper oxide)		(carbon monoxide)		(copper)		(carbon dioxide)

This work has been duplicated in Austria (Böhne 1968) and recent observations of copper smelting in Africa have tended to confirm the suitability of these simple techniques in producing copper.

The working of copper and bronze into tools and other articles

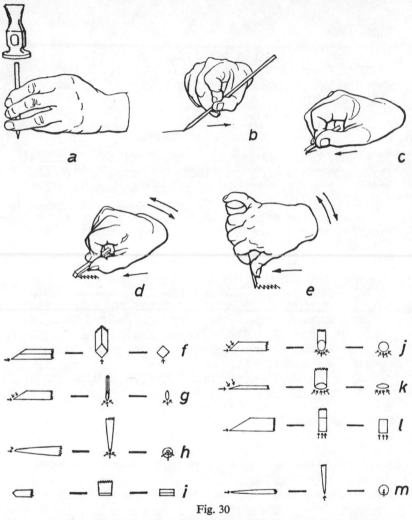

Fig. 30

Tools and techniques of working bronze (from Lowery, Savage and Wilkins 1971)

a, i	Tracing or chasing of metal
b, m	Scribing preliminary marks on metal
c, f–h, j, k	Graving, removal of metal
d, e, l	Scorping, removal of metal in quantity

has been the subject of many experiments. Some have concerned the shaping of metal by beating, and its embellishment, others have involved casting in moulds. A series of experiments in the decoration of sheet and cast bronzes has shown the range of tools and techniques which craftsmen could employ (Fig. 30) and the variety of ornamentive marks which can be recognised on ancient metals (Pl. 14) (Lowery, Savage and Wilkins 1971).

Copper melts at 1083°C, and a 10 per cent tin bronze melts at about 1000°C; both are considerably higher than a campfire temperature. In casting experiments in ancient moulds, bronze was used (Voce 1951). One piece of a bivalve stone mould for a sickle from Lake Zurich was matched with a reverse-image replica, and both were dried at 150°C before pouring a 7 per cent tin bronze at 1150°C. The mould remained undamaged, and the casting was of good appearance.

A bronze bivalve mould for a palstave, from France, was also used. It was heated to 150°C for drying before the bronze was poured at 1150°C, and the resulting palstave was of excellent quality. No damage to the bronze mould was recorded, and this was probably the most significant result, that the sudden introduction of metal at 1150°C did not alter the metal of the mould.

Rather more concern has been recently attached to the alteration of certain elements within a bronze metal through heating and casting (Slater and Charles 1970). Many coppers contain small trace elements of impurities, lead, silver, iron, bismuth, antimony, arsenic, and so on, and in analyses of ancient implements these elements are used to relate material to each other and to its source. Experimental work, still underway, has shown that some of these elements, bismuth and lead, may segregate during melting and cooling in copper, and therefore their absolute proportions can differ within a single object.

Another type of mould, for complex designs, is the one-piece clay mould modelled around a lead or wax model, heated to fire the clay and melt the model, and broken to extract the cast metal object. The technique is employed, in modern versions, for rapid production of metal castings. Among experiments in casting ancient objects by this lost-wax or cire-perdue method, one was based upon a sixteenth-century account of the casting of gold and silver bells (Long 1965). In the tests, copper was used in place of gold, in an attempt to show that the method described was feasible for baser metals. The melting temperature for gold is 1063°C, that for copper 1083°C, but the major difference lies in the tendency of copper to absorb oxygen when in a molten state, and therefore to produce a porous imperfect casting.

The object selected for replication was a cast copper bell from a prehistoric site in Mexico, of the first millennium A.D. (Fig. 31). The sixteenth-century record indicated that the mould had consisted of a mixture of clay and charcoal, the model was of beeswax,

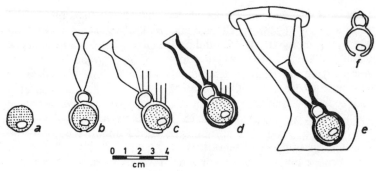

Fig. 31

Stages in the production of a copper bell with pebble clapper (after Long 1964)

    a Clay and charcoal core with pebble
    b Wax model of bell and stem
    c Model angled with straw vents in place
    d Model coated with clay and charcoal paste
    e Outer clay and charcoal coating, reservoir and cap
    f Finished product

with white copal to aid its shaping. These substances or nearest equivalents were used in the experiment. A small core of charcoal and clay was made containing a pebble, the bell clapper; wax was pressed around the core in the thickness and shape of the bell, and a wax ring or handle attached. A wax stem was fixed to the upper part of the handle to provide a reservoir of molten metal during the casting, cooling and shrinking of the copper; there was no evidence for this in the aboriginal objects, but it would help in a minor way, and would absorb gases. A slit was cut in the bottom of the wax bell, so that the application of the clay and charcoal covering, forming the mould, would fill this and hold the core in place when the wax was melted out; several straws were also pushed through the upper part of the wax bell, to later burn or be pulled out and allow trapped air to escape. Several coatings of ground charcoal and clay and water were brushed onto the wax and dried for 2 days, then covered by charcoal and clay to make the mould body firm; a crucible of the same was attached to the top of the stem, the whole inclined to one side, so that the metal would flow in one side, forcing the air out through the vents in the other until the copper rose to block them. Before heating, pieces of copper were placed in the crucible and a clay and charcoal cap sealed this. After drying, the whole structure was placed in a wind draught furnace filled with 4·5 kg of charcoal, and heated to approximately

1200°C. The wax bell and stem reservoir were melted out and vaporised, the copper was melted and flowed down into the mould, where it formed the metal bell. The outer core was broken, the metal stem removed, and the clay-charcoal core inside the bell was chipped out with an awl, leaving the pebble clapper in place. The bell had only to be polished.

The procedures and results almost exactly followed the sixteenth-century description for gold, and conformed to good metallurgical principles; the results seemed to justify the claim that the sixteenth-century record only slightly disguised a useful statement on copper casting of intricate objects.

Gold and silver objects from ancient times have always created great interest among not only prehistorians but also the general public. Their beauty, their generally excellent state of preservation, their current antique value, all combine to make them objects of curiosity and envy. Few attempts have been made, or allowed, to determine the ways by which they were manufactured, as these attempts usually involve some destruction of the metal. One approach to this difficulty is through reproducing, in equivalent metal, precious objects so that they may be compared visually, and the model subjected to destructive examination.

Among the more spectacular ornaments of gold recovered in recent years from Britain are the 6 gold torcs from Ipswich, dating to the first century B.C. Each weighs about 1000 grams, and the maximum diameter is about 19 cm. They are of 60–89 per cent gold, 10–27 per cent silver, and 0–12 per cent copper. One experiment has attempted to show how these torcs were made (Brailsford and Stapley 1972). The wires for the body are 8-sided, and were replicated by pouring Fine Silver into a groove cut in a wood block, then shaping in an iron swage of 3 facets and 2 half-facets. The rod was turned to complete the octagonal section, and the flashes of metal beaten out along the facet junctions were cut off. The ends of the wire were worked into tapers, and the wire was bent like a hairpin. The two free ends were gripped in a vice, and a wooden rod was put through the looped end and twisted, to twist the wires into the torc shape. Annealing during swaging and twisting was needed to prevent the metal becoming too brittle. The terminals of the Ipswich torcs were modelled first in wax, attached to the wire body, and then invested in plaster. After heating, the wax was drained off and Fine Silver poured in to fuse with the body and form the elaborate decoration. The actual experimental result was a partial failure due to overheating of the mould, but the overall result showed the feasibility of the method, and the various process marks were in accordance with those on the actual torcs themselves.

Many of the tools used in the production of gold and bronze objects, and many larger implements for agricultural or other industrial pursuits, were made of iron from about 600 B.C. in the British Isles. The sources of iron ore were far more abundant than those of copper and tin, and allowed a greater exploitation by more people of the available metallic materials. The processes by which ore was reduced to a workable state have been examined by many experiments based upon the excavated remains of ancient smelting furnaces.

A simple bowl furnace, reconstructed from a Great Casterton, Rutland, furnace of Roman date, was tested and found capable of reducing ores although the iron yield was low (Wynne and Tylecote 1958). The original smelting hearth was 1·2 metres diameter and 0·45 metre deep; charcoal and reddened clay lined the bowl within which was a slab of slag with unroasted ore filling the upper part. The reconstruction was based upon these remains, with the addition of recording devices. The ore was calcined at 800°C in an oxidising atmosphere before the smelt. Charcoal was ignited in the furnace, and gradually alternate layers of ore and charcoal were added. About 4 hours were required for a layer of ore to pass down into the hearth at base, during which time it was reduced by carbon monoxide. Charcoal was added after all the ore had passed down in order to separate slag and metal. An alternative method was tried, with all the ore packed into the hearth before firing the charcoal (Fig. 32a). The result of the tests was a yield of compacted iron, much slag and some reduced iron ore (Fig. 32b). The weight of the slag and ore was greater than twice the iron, and the maximum efficiency was a yield of 0·34 kg of iron from 1·8 kg of ore, 20 per cent.

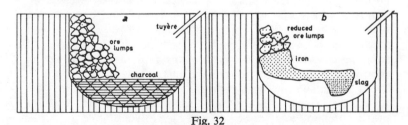

Fig. 32
Bowl furnace (after Wynne and Tylecote 1958)
a With pre-packed ore
b After smelting

A reconstruction of an Iron Age smelting furnace in Denmark was based upon a furnace shaft from north Germany, and slag blocks often found in pits (Voss 1962). A clay shaft was erected over a pit in the ground, with 4 holes providing air near the base of the shaft; the chimney effect of the shaft would ensure a suitable supply of air (Fig. 33*a*). The slag pit held a straw plug which closed

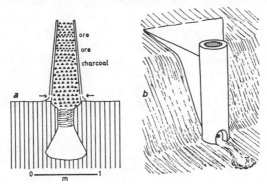

Fig. 33

a Reconstruction of iron-smelting furnace with slag pit beneath straw and twig plug (after Voss 1962)

b Reconstruction of the Ashwicken, Norfolk, shaft furnace with clay platform outside slag tap hole and tuyere at base, and slag drain (after Tylecote and Owles 1960)

off the pit from the shaft; this plug could be held in place by wooden sticks, or by setting it on a clay cylinder rising from the bottom of the pit. In either case, the plug would hold up the slag, and after a suitable time the slag would burn through and run into or be pushed into the pit. The metallic iron formed in the furnace would be spongy and stick to the shaft sides or fall to the bottom. This form of furnace is basic to other experiments involving firing processes, and one of these, at Varde Steelworks in Jutland, using a reconstructed fourth–fifth century A.D. shaft furnace, successfully produced metal (Tylecote 1969).

At Ashwicken, Norfolk, 6 shaft furnaces were recovered by excavation, and one of these was reconstructed (Tylecote and Owles 1961). The furnaces, of the second century A.D., were tall and narrow, and were probably made by coating a tree trunk with clay and then firing it, repeating the process until a wall 20 cm thick had been built up when the carbonised wood could be removed. A hole at the base allowed slag to be tapped out and collected in a hollow in the sand (Fig. 33*b*). The reconstruction used firebrick for the walls, and it was found that 8 hours were needed to heat the furnace up to smelting temperature of 1200°C using the induced air from the high chimney draught. The maximum smelting experiment of 8 hours produced 3·5 kg of iron and, from this and from the archaeological remains, it was considered that a run of 24 hours was likely, consuming 45 kg of charcoal, processing 35 kg of ore and producing 13·5 kg of raw bloom.

Other reconstructed furnaces have also been tested experimentally. A Romano-British shaft furnace based on an excavated example at Holbeanwood, Sussex, produced up to 9 kg of iron at one firing, and proved to be durable and probably capable of 10 or 12 smelts before repairs were necessary (Cleere 1970).

These experiments in iron-smelting have tended to show that the process could be accomplished in various ways without much difficulty. The archaeological remains of Iron Age, Roman and Germanic Iron Ages in northern and western Europe demonstrate a basic similarity in the technique of iron-smelting, and they can and have been compared directly with the surviving elements of smelting furnaces in other regions of the world, Africa in particular, where very closely comparable shaft furnaces in particular are still or were recently in use (Robinson 1961; Voss 1962). Our understanding of ancient smelting processes has been amplified considerably by both experiment and ethnography.

HIDES, LEATHERS AND TEXTILES

The widespread use of hides and leathers in prehistoric times, like that of textiles, is an archaeological assumption. Relatively little of these materials has survived, as it is only under exceptional conditions, principally waterlogging, that decay has not been total. The rapid disintegration of these substances in the Overton Down earthwork illustrates how complete our loss of knowledge is about ancient clothing. Some few traces remain, however, and illustrate how extensive and varied were the personal garments of prehistoric people; leather jerkins, woollen cloaks and corded skirts have survived in places, and representations of humans as stone and clay figurines also indicate types of clothing and decoration. Other archaeological evidence consists of tools for working hides, and parts of looms for weaving textiles.

Ancient textiles are a specialised study, and recent work has shown how intricate designs were incorporated into cloths. Few experiments have been made to test how such looms operated, but the difficulty is that the surviving evidence is sparse; post holes for the loom stand, loom weights, spindle whorls, presumptive weaving combs, and a few parts of collapsed looms are all that remain. One experiment on a simple loom was conducted to show how such an object might have looked, and to test if the positioning of the loom within a hut seriously affected the light and therefore the performance of the weaver (Reynolds 1972). The bone comb proved to be highly successful in pushing the weft into place before it was beaten by the sword, and little difference in the quality of the textiles produced within and without the hut was noted. Clearly much more experimental work on weaving appliances could be done, but, on the other hand, specialised observations of ancient textiles can go a long way towards deducing the precise type of weaving procedures used (Wild 1970; Henshall 1950).

For leathers and hides of early times, certain problems remain to be solved by observation and analysis, as well as by testing of replicated objects. The acquisition of hides is of course a first step, and many demonstrations have been carried out on the skinning of deer and other animals with flint flakes and other more sophisticated knives (Leakey 1954; Swauger and Wallace 1964; Shafer 1971); all have tended to show how effective an unretouched flint can be, possessing a sharp slightly serrated edge that cuts in a sawing motion through animal fibre with great ease. A small deer could be skinned in about 15 minutes.

The preparation of hides for tanning processes, in beam-house operations, are well-known, and the use of rib bones for this has been noted (p. 130). Only analysis will show if vegetable or oil tanning was used on ancient hides, and no experiments on these have been documented adequately. One experiment involving leather, with the additional problem of reversing its usual main attraction of flexibility, was concerned with the production and testing of shields.

One of the features of the Late Bronze Age in the British Isles is the appearance not only of hill-forts but also of slashing and sticking swords in great profusion. The same phenomena appear on the continent and it seems that from about 900 B.C. there was some unrest, some movement of groups of people, and some forms of conflict or fear of conflict. Along with the swords, in the British Isles in particular, appear shields of sheet bronze, of wood and of leather. On the continent there are various pieces of sheet-bronze armour as well.

The bronze shields are often elaborately decorated with ribs and bosses, numbering several hundreds, and the effort taken in their production must have been considerable. The metal sheet is extremely thin, 2–4mm, and it has always been uncertain if such fragile objects would serve as defensive shields in actual conflict, or if shields of wood or leather would have been in general use. Only one leather shield of the Late Bronze Age has survived, and an experiment was mounted to reproduce both metal and leather shields and to test their capabilities (Coles 1962).

The experimental production of leather shields was based upon the sole surviving example of such an object from Clonbrin, Co. Longford, Ireland. This shield, found in 1908 during peat-cutting, was 50cm in diameter and 5–6mm thick. It had a handle laced onto the back and was without doubt complete; there were no traces of any wood or metal fastenings or supports. The shield had a central boss and three concentric ribs, the outer two of which had a V-shaped notch; there were also several groups of small bosses between the ribs. On the basis of this decoration, the shield was dated to about the eighth century B.C.

The original publication of this find accepted the widespread belief that hide shields of Roman times tended to collapse in wet conditions: 'shields of bull's hide . . . were useless at close quarters because they were flexible rather than firm; and when their leather shrunk and rotted from the rain, unserviceable as they were before, they then became entirely so' (Ridgeway, 1901, 468–9, quoting Polybius). In fact, however, Roman auxiliaries' shields were made of wood, covered with hide or leather and bound with metal strips at the edges; as such, they would have withstood not only force but rain, both conditions no doubt present over much of the British Isles.

Studies of ancient hides and leathers had concentrated upon the most valuable properties of the material, their strength and flexibility. For shields of the Bronze Age, however, lacking any backing of wood or metal, the flexible nature of leather would have been the main problem to be overcome. The experimental production of leather shields was directed primarily at this problem. First, however, the nature of the material to be tested had to be determined.

The skin or hide of animals consists of three layers, the outer layer or epidermis, the middle layer or corium, the inner layer of flesh or adipose tissue. Leather is made from the middle layer, after the removal by soaking, kneading, sweating and scraping of the inner and outer layers. The true skin thus left consists principally of the protein collagen, composed of fibrils, fibres and fibre-bundles, all held together by a tissue structure. This combination gives hide its unique character, strong yet flexible.

In a dry climate, a hide could be used without tanning into leather, as putrefaction might be very slow; early Egyptian examples of raw-hide objects exist, and American Indians have been observed making raw-hide shields by pegging a buffalo hide over a mound of sand and then toasting the dried shield to toughen it. But damp conditions would start to soften and to decay such products; there seemed no reason to suggest that the Irish shield could have been made of raw-hide, buried as it was in a peatbog. A small fragment of the prehistoric shield was analysed and this suggested that the hide was probably cattle-skin that had been vegetable tanned; available materials would have included oak, chestnut and pine bark, and oak galls. For the experimental production of shields, the shoulder portions of heavy domestic cattle hides were obtained; these were vegetable tanned, but had also been 'oiled off', their surface spread with oil while wet to maintain flexibility. It is likely that Bronze Age methods of tanning were less concentrated than those of today, and possibly a very slight tanning would have prevented putrefaction; the analyses did not define this more closely. The major problems remained, how to shape and retain the shield form in damp conditions.

Various experiments were carried out on leathers of the appropriate thickness and shape. A wooden mould was made, based on two surviving Bronze Age moulds from Ireland, forming a flat surface into which were cut a central depression (for the boss), and concentric grooves (for the ribs). The leather was then soaked in cold water for two hours and scrubbed with a wooden slat; this removed most of the tanning material that might remain in the grain of the leather as excess matter. The presence of this prevents full flexibility of the leather during its shaping in the mould, and may then cause cracks to appear, technically 'bursters'. After draining for four hours, the leather was placed over the mould and pushed into the central depression and grooves with a series of wooden round-ended punches; this was an extremely easy operation, so long as the leather in the central hollow was held firm by weights as the grooves were filled by punching and scrubbing the leather into them. This process took no more than three minutes. Weighted wooden slats were placed over the shield in its mould, to hold it in place, and it was then allowed to dry at inside temperatures of 10°–15°C. During the drying, the leather tended to shrink and it had to be beaten back into its grooves every four hours for 3 days, after which time the shield was removed, and allowed to dry out on its front for a week. The total shrinkage was only 3 per cent, and the shield was fairly hard yet still slightly flexible. A handle, formed of an end-tongued piece, turned in and laced, was attached across the central dome by leather thongs. The product was functional as a shield, but would soften in damp conditions.

Five experiments with leather shields were then carried out, in attempts to harden the leather and make it water resistant. The basic method was heat, using water or wax. It seemed likely that beeswax could have been used in ancient times for impregnation, although there is no certain evidence for this, so the first test was to decide if paraffin wax could be substituted for the less-available beeswax; small pieces of leather were dipped in beeswax or in paraffin wax and their resulting appearances did not differ. One shield was then immersed in hot paraffin wax, at 71°C, until bubbling ceased after 4 minutes; it was then extracted, in a softened condition, drained and dried naturally. The result was a shield of a high gloss, brown in colour, almost totally inflexible, and impervious to water-soaking.

The other method of stiffening shields was by heat. Four shields were tested, one by dipping in a hot water bath (80°C) for 30 seconds. The result was a shield hard yet slightly flexible, and resistant to severe water soaking. Repeated tests using this method showed that control of water temperature and time was crucial to the method. Another shield was roasted in an oven at 70°–80°C for 2 minutes; shrinkage then set in and the rescued product was satisfactory if a little uneven. A third shield had hot water poured over its faces, both front and back. The water was near to boiling, and it was necessary to keep the water running over and off the shield to avoid shrinkage. The result was a stiffened shield that withstood a light but not prolonged soaking by rain. The fourth shield was formed differently; a piece of leather was dipped in a hot bath at 80°C for $1\frac{1}{4}$ minutes and then beaten into the wooden mould. Shrinkage tests had been carried out on different pieces of leather and the timing was acute, any delay in beating causing drastic and irredeemable shrinkage and distortion. This method seemed difficult to control and it is unlikely to have been used in prehistoric times. The other methods all gave satisfactory results, and in the absence of any evidence of wax on the Clonbrin shield, some stiffening by heated water seemed the most likely ancient method.

This experiment was then continued by the manufacture of metal shields. Two copies of metal shields were made, based upon examination of many of the bronze shields of the European Bronze Age. The copies were made of copper sheet, as bronze sheet was unobtainable at the time. The thickness of the metal (3 mm) was comparable to that of ancient examples, and in the beating of the central boss and ribs, the hardness of the metal approached that of the genuine articles (Vickers Pyramid hardness: copy 88–92, original 93). There was no need to anneal the metal during the beating process. A handle was riveted onto one of the shields, and, for added strength, a bronze wire was enclosed within the turned rim of the shield, matching one or two ancient examples but not the majority.

Two shields, one water-hardened leather, the other of beaten metal, were then subjected to a series of tests designed to show if either or both could stand up to physical attack (Pl. 16). A bronze spearhead on a shaft punctured the metal shield, and the first slash with a Bronze Age sword cut the shield almost in two, only the wired rim holding the parts together. The leather shield was then subjected to the same attack, and the spear barely perforated the leather; the sword was used with vigour and the shield resisted 15 blows, the only damage being a series of slight cuts in the outer surface of the leather. The flexibility of the shield absorbed and deflected the blows.

The conclusion of the experiment was that leather shields were likely to have served a functional use as protective devices if they were so required in the Late Bronze Age, but bronze shields, and body armour too, so often found in peatbogs and rivers, were likely to have been objects of display and parade, perhaps deliberately deposited in lakes and streams, but unlikely to have ever been relied upon for body protection.

POTTERY MANUFACTURE

The invention of pottery occurred as long ago as 25000 years, in the discovery by late glacial man that small figurines could be modelled in clay and hardened in a camp fire. It is perhaps surprising that it was not until 7000 B.C. that pottery vessels for containing water and for heating liquid foods were first manufactured, in the Middle East. Thereafter, independently in many cases, pottery vessels were produced throughout much of the Old and the New World, and today they represent one of the two most abundant materials recovered from archaeological sites. Ancient pottery varies from thick coarse wares, poorly prepared and inadequately fired, to fine, thin, decorated wares exhibiting all the sophistication in techniques that a potter could bring to bear upon his clay. Experiments in the field of pottery manufacture have inadequately covered the range, but certain classes have been extensively examined, and some tests have been conducted on certain basic features of pots.

In a primary series of experiments, modern clays were used to replicate prehistoric pottery, so that analyses of the two could be compared (Hodges 1962). The two major results from this study were that the minerals in the clay could be identified and therefore some ideas obtained about its source, and that the techniques of pottery-making in ancient times, methods of construction, surfacing, and firing conditions, could be better understood. Examination and analysis of pottery had of course been a feature of much archaeological study prior to this, but the experimental approach had only been previously applied to specific problems and not to overall theoretical assumptions.

It was found that ring-built and coil-built pottery could in some cases be indistinguishable from single lump wheel-thrown pottery, as the junctions between the rings might be totally obscured in shaping and firing; identifications of sections of pottery yielding no evidence of ring- and coil-building need not therefore necessarily dispose of this method of manufacture.

Potsherds were also made and fired without surfacing materials, with hand slurry of water and clay, and with a white clay slip; the results were then compared with a Beaker sherd, claimed to have been slipped, but which did not resemble at all the slipped experimental sherd. The conclusion was that it must have been rapid firing at a high temperature that brought out to the surface of the Beaker the breakdown of clay minerals giving the false impression of a slip.

A series of experimental firings of sherds was conducted to investigate the quantity and location of unburnt carbon within the sherd, and the presence of altered clay minerals. It was found that the more porous was the fabric, the more readily was carbon burnt out, and that under extreme reducing conditions (a kiln with damp sawdust), little carbon was burnt out, whereas under extreme oxidising conditions (an electric kiln with no sawdust), all of the carbon was burnt out. Intermediate experiments were carried out and it was concluded that the nature of the wood used was as important as the shape of the kiln in ancient times. The duration of firing was tested, and it was shown that prolonged firing removed all carbon, but only high temperatures would alter the minerals. The rate of firing was then tested, and it was shown that just as the temperature in a bonfire rises quickly and cools slowly, so sherds fired in this way had surface minerals altered by heat, but the inner part still had carbon unconsumed; when fired in lower temperatures, the carbon was removed totally, but the minerals were unaltered.

These experimental results were then compared with a series of prehistoric sherds from Britain. Beaker sherds, with much carbon burnt out, and clay minerals only altered on the surface, suggested firing in strongly oxidising conditions but with high temperatures not maintained for long, that is, in a brushwood bonfire. Neolithic sherds, on the other hand, contained much carbon and the clay minerals were not altered, thus suggesting firing at a lower temperature in medium (reducing-oxidising) conditions, such as a fire fed by logs and not branches.

In a study of pottery from second millennium B.C. Indian settlements in Georgia, USA., experimental work was done on making and firing pottery in attempts to duplicate the fibre-tempered reddish wares (Williams 1968, 320). It was found that Spanish moss provided the tempering medium, and that under reducing conditions the colour of the replicated wares was identical to that of the originals.

A major class of pottery that has been subjected to exhaustive and continuing experimental work is Romano-British coarse ware, and this illustrates one of the requirements of experimental work, that it should be continuous and built upon previous work. The success of recent experiments in producing this ware owes much to the less successful initial attempts.

Pottery manufacture was a major industry in Roman Britain, and many factories have been located and excavated, and their products traced over exchange networks. The precise nature of the kilns and firing methods for such a large industry has been a subject of concern for archaeologists, because it seems likely that some form of mass-production process must have been used in which kilns requiring much building and repair, and techniques yielding no guarantee of success, probably played little part.

One of the earliest experiments in building and testing a kiln was conducted at Boston, Lincs., on a replica of the Water Newton kiln (Mayes 1961). This type consisted of a cylindrical hole in the ground lined with clay, fired clay blocks or stones coated with clay. A flue led into the lower part of the kiln cylinder from a stoke-hole. Inside the kiln was a clay pedestal or tongue at a level consistent with a ledge around the side of the cylinder, the whole supporting a perforated clay floor on which the clay pots rested. Some form of covering was put over this part, the oven, when the pots were in place.

The Boston oven was about one metre in internal diameter and could have been built by 2 men in 3 days if clay was available to hand. It was dried out, pre-fired, and then loaded with 182 pots, mostly upside-down, in layers. Grass was placed over the pots, and a dome of clay and sticks, with vents, was built over all. The firing operation consumed 2 tonnes of wood, and temperatures of 1000°C were reached after 12 hours; when the flue and dome vents were sealed by clay the slow cooling took 30 hours, after which the dome was removed and the pottery unloaded. Some of the pots had slipped and been damaged; others had cooled too rapidly, but over 100 were successful products although they were oxidised by the presence of oxygen during cooling. The kiln was damaged but could have been repaired.

The lessons learned from this work were applied to a second test at Boston (Mayes 1962), when far fewer pots were wasters, most pots were reduced and black in colour, the consumption of fuel had been reduced by half, and the kiln would have needed only minor repairs before re-firing.

The experimental work on Romano-British kilns had up to this point concentrated on producing a single firing of reduced pottery. Further work was aimed at multiple firings and the problem of kiln roofing.

A kiln built of estuarine clays at Barton-on-Humber, Lincs., to the same basic plan (Pl. 17) was considered to represent about 30 hours of work by an experienced kiln-maker; in the reconstruction it took 99 man-hours (Bryant 1970). It was pre-fired 6 days before firing the pottery. A total of 78 pots were loaded in, and after 11 hours and 225 kg of wood, the temperature inside reached 1010°C; at this point the kiln was sealed with a metal plate and clay slurry over the oven vent. The fire was pushed into the kiln, and logs into the flue, and then it too was bricked up at the entry. Water was poured down a pipe, normally used for sampling the kiln gases, to build up pressure within the kiln and prevent oxygen entering. After 7 hours, and a temperature fall of 100°C per hour, the kiln was opened. Most of the pots had fired perfectly except for a group made of Kimmeridge clay alone, and most were non-oxidised. The kiln was fired again, after minor filling of cracks, and water was not added during the firing; the pots again were non-oxidised. A third firing was attempted, after rebuilding the flue arch, and a longer cooling period of 13 hours was allowed; all the pots were non-oxidised and were far blacker than in the first two firings. The valuable conclusion was that repeated firings actually produced a more air-tight kiln.

Attention was then directed to the domes over the ovens, which had previously been clay-built and more or less permanent in appearance (cf. Brightwell *et al.* 1972), although some efforts had been made to fire with temporary domes of turf and clay slabs. Two more kilns were built at Barton-on-Humber, one with an exposed free-standing wall (Fig. 34), the other buried in a bank of

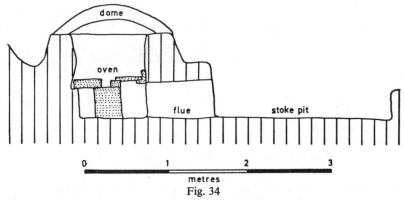

Fig. 34

Section through experimental Romano-British kiln at Barton-on-Humber, Lincs. (after Bryant 1971)

the Humber river (Bryant 1971). After pre-firing, the pots were loaded in, and a fire lit and pushed into the flue. After 4 hours the temperature had reached 500°C within the oven. Sixteen clay plates, fired, were then put over the load, followed by pieces of tile to block any holes, and turfs which were laid in 2 rows around the roof edge, leaving a central vent ·3 m wide. The high temperatures (up to 800°C) did not endanger the workers during this operation. Clay was packed over the turfs and after a total of 9·5 hours firing the vent was sealed with turf and clay, and the flue blocked. Only 250 kg of wood was used for the operation, and after 8 hours cooling the kiln was opened. Of 94 pots, only 8 were wasters, and 90 were completely non-oxidised. The results of this test with the free-standing kiln were not duplicated with the buried kiln due to incorrect placing of the flue.

The conclusions of all these experiments with Romano-British kilns, each test building on the results of the previous one, are that kiln-building and firing is relatively easy, requiring some experience in positioning of flue arches, that fuel consumption is low, and that loading of pots is no problem. The use of broken tiles and turfs and clay is a safe substitute for a permanent clay dome. The re-use of kilns seems to help provide the right conditions for the production of non-oxidised pottery. These experiments then have added appreciably to our understanding of the technical processes used by Romano-British potters, and therefore to our knowledge of the organisation of the pottery industry in the first millennium A.D.

The production of other types of pottery has also been attempted, but particular concern has been given to wares from the Classical world of the Mediterranean and from ancient Egypt. Unglazed but glossy black wares from Etruria and many other areas were first reproduced experimentally by Mercer in Pennsylvania (MacIver 1921). Small vessels were made and rubbed with red ochre, then burnished with a piece of smooth glass (a pebble would have done as well); the pots were then placed in an open fire-place and covered by fuel. After firing, the polish and the red colour had been retained. Black glossy pots were produced in the same way by burnishing, but without adding the ochre.

A variation on this, the production of black-topped ware with red bodies, an Egyptian feature, was also produced by Mercer in one operation. A pot of ferruginous clay, which would burn red in a clear fire, was rubbed with red ochre and then burnished. The pot was dried and then placed upside down with the rim buried in a layer of sawdust. A wire net covered the pot and protected it from contact with the straw fuel for the fire which burned for 45 minutes. After cooling the pot was seen to be red-bodied, with a black rim, duplicating the ancient Egyptian examples.

An alternative method, using two operations, was tested by Lucas (1962, 380). Damp pots were coated with a wash of red ochre, polished with a quartz pebble, dried and baked in a furnace; still red-hot, they were then placed upside down with rims buried in sawdust. The result was black-topped pots, which had clear red bodies if the sawdust or straw could be kept from smoking too much; a covering of sand would prevent this.

More elaborate, highly decorated pots are a feature of the Classical world. *Terra sigillata* red and Greek black wares, both glossy in appearance but not glazed, were recognised in the last century as identical in composition, the colour difference caused by firing in non-oxidising conditions for retention of black iron oxide colouring, and firing in oxidising conditions for alteration of black to red ferric oxide.

The gloss on pottery of these types was not fully understood until experimental work was done on materials found by analysis to be present in the clays. Samples of kaolinite, montmorillonite and a muscovite-type were made into slips, painted onto sherds and fired at 1000°C. The first two gave dull layers, but the third, called illite, produced both shine and colour of *terra sigillata* (Bimson 1956). The regional distribution of this pottery in the continent could then be related to the sources of the particular clays containing illite, sources that were clearly highly valued.

The work on Greek black and *terra sigillata* wares therefore showed that basically they were the same. The gloss is obtained by painting the partly dried pot with a suspension of illite clay containing some iron. When fired in oxidising conditions, *terra sigillata* red is produced, but if exposed to reducing gases then black ware is produced.

The point has been emphasised that this form of surface decoration is a gloss and not a true glaze. Glaze is, strictly speaking, a vitreous layer covering earthenware or porcelain, and occurs on certain ancient Egyptian wares. Experiments have been conducted in attempts to discover the nature of this process, and the materials used. The ingredients of ancient blue glazes were an alkali, a small proportion of copper compound, calcium carbonate and much silica. Tests with malachite and alkali were made, and by heating potassium carbonate (the alkali, obtained from wood and plant ash) or powdered natron (see p. 134), mixed with powdered malachite, on silica-rich quartz pebbles, a blue glaze was obtained (Lucas 1962, 172). There was no need to add any other silica or calcium carbonate, and by further work it was found possible to glaze powdered quartz which led to the successful reproduction of Egyptian faience; this involved first glazing solid quartz, then chipping off and powdering the glaze, finally covering the moulded powdered quartz object (bead, etc.) with the powdered glaze, and heating. This is possibly the method used in ancient times, but its use is not entirely certain. A simpler method, described as a one-stage process, has recently been discovered (Wulff *et al.* 1968).

Decoration on ancient pottery was more easily applied by impressing sticks, bones and fingers into the wet clay, and much prehistoric pottery has a bewildering array of impressed decoration, a busy field for archaeological studies. The actual equipment used for the impressions has not been so often studied, and one of the first studies was the recognition that British Neolithic pottery bore imprints of a wide range of bird bone (Liddell 1929). Experiments showed that the variety of impressions that could be made with the leg-bones and larger wing-bones of a blackbird (*Merula merula*) was over 100, and that other bird bones also showed a great range, some of which exactly fitted the impressions on Neolithic pottery of the third millennium B.C. More elaborate impressing tools would have been manufactured to specific or experimental designs by native potters, and some of these tools have been used to decorate replicas of ancient pottery. Circular bone rouletting tools from Hopewell sites in Kansas and adjacent areas are known, and were used like miniature wheels to impress marks on wet clay pots; the edges of the discs are notched in various ways. A curved notched tool from a site in Ohio was used to decorate, in rocking fashion, part of a facsimile Hopewell pot and the result was closely comparable to the decoration on genuine Hopewell vessels (Quimby 1949). Plasticine has often been used to receive the imprints of tools such as these, and to demonstrate stages in the modelling of clay figurines, but these do not really fall within the compass of the experimental work treated here (e.g. Drucker 1952, 132; Braunholtz 1934).

The experiments in the manufacturing processes of ancient pottery are numerous, and have demonstrated the ease with which such products were produced and decorated. The value of kilns for both the firing of pottery and for the smelting and casting of metal would no doubt have contributed to the rapid development of these furnaces into efficient structures. The use of some of these for the baking and smoking of food has also been noted (p. 48). The continued experiments with Romano-British kilns have demonstrated the extreme importance in undertaking a series of tests, and in developing a fuller understanding of the processes involved through collaboration and assessment of previous work; this is perhaps one of the strongest arguments for the establishment of a central body of data and support for experimental archaeology.

PAINTING AND PAPER

Paintings and engravings were first produced 35000 years ago, insofar as the archaeological record can tell us. The drawings of animals, sub-humans, and other designs, on the walls of shelters and caves in southern France and northern Spain represent the first artistic expressions of ancient man that have survived. These have been the subject of much concern about their ritual or other significance in recent years, and few attempts have been made to simulate the conditions under which they were produced. Laboratory replication of paintings and engravings have been made, but no one seems to have undertaken the more valuable task of working within the caverns under prehistoric conditions of light and heat; no consistent estimates of the time involved in the decoration of a wall panel, or an entire cave, have been made. Of course this would not lead to a greater understanding of the meaning of the art, as the perceptual capabilities of ancient man are beyond recall.

Both paintings and engravings have on occasion been reproduced for purposes of display. Miles Burkitt of Cambridge experimented with ochres and charcoals, using brushes of horsehair mounted on bird-bone handles, split long bones for holding paints, a scapula for a palette, and a stone lamp with suet and a moss wick. He found that the mixing of paint, the provision of light at the correct 'angle', and the actual painting, were rather complicated for one man alone in a darkened room, and he thought that an apprentice helper would have been required by the late glacial artists working in the caves of France and Spain. He also worked with flint burins on replica limestone walls, and found that different widths and depths could be made by turning a single burin, and that lighting held accurately and in different positions was essential. It is possible, he considered, that these situations were responsible for the stylistic continuity apparent in certain areas, that the helper holding the lamp or mixing the paints would absorb some of the master's stylistic tricks and when he eventually replaced his teacher, the style would continue. This theory depends, of course, on many other considerations about the art and its meaning, and is certainly not, nor did Miles Burkitt consider it to be, proved, but it remains an interesting contribution to the subject.

Some few caves in this area contain representations of human hands, and many of these are negative impressions, the paint having been applied around a hand held against a wall. Some of the hands, notably those from Gargas in the Pyrenees, lack joints of some fingers (Fig. 35a–c), and there has been much speculation

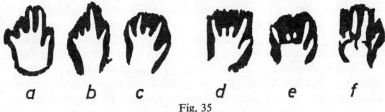

a   b   c   d   e   f

Fig. 35

Silhouettes of hands (after Sollas 1915)
a–c from the cave of Gargas, Pyrenees, late glacial
d–f Experimentally produced: d by sifting rouge, e by blowing charcoal from the mouth, f by blowing rouge from a tube

and testing of the theory that it was not possible to produce the impression if the joints had merely been bent under and not actually removed by cutting. One experiment was conducted by Sollas in trying to reproduce the mutilated hands without disposing of any fingers (1915, 354). A hand was placed on paper, with a finger joint bent under, and a crayon, such as an ochre pencil, was used to trace the outline. Another method tried was to fill the mouth with charcoal and puff it against the hand; one attempt was made but the experimenters were not disposed to more practice in this clearly messy and unpleasant procedure. Powdered rouge, in place of ochre, was also blown through a tube, and sifted over a hand held flat, and all of these methods produced an impression of a hand lacking finger-joints (Fig. 35*d–f*). The conclusion was that whatever cult it was that prompted late glacial man to make representations of mutilated hands, he did not in fact have to actually remove the joints to make an adequate impression.

An experiment of a more basic type was undertaken in South Africa to discover the nature of the pigments and mixing media used in the numerous painted rock shelters of the region (Johnson 1957). Much of this painting (Pl. 18), and engraving as well, is attributed to Bushmen hunter-gatherers who occupied the most favourable territories until the arrival of European settlers and others. In the experimental reproduction of the colours, only locally available pigments and media were used.

The colours included sienna (compounds of iron and manganese), white (oxides of metal such as non-local zinc, white earth kaolin, bird droppings), yellow (clays stained with iron oxide, yielding also red), black (charcoal black), and brown (like sienna).

The media used in the experimental paintings were varied. Wax resin required a heated palette, as the wax and ochre dried quickly, and no fine lines could be produced by the paste. Marrow fat and ochre made more paste, suitable for wide lines and area-painting, and when applied the result recalled certain red and black paintings nearby. Hyrax urine was not tried, as no hyrax would co-operate; the droppings, however, were tried without success. Mutton fat proved difficult, probably fading in time, and fine lines were not successfully drawn. Various juices from plants would not mix with enough density to give a useful colour, and large quantities were needed. Gall-bladder bile was a possible source of medium but its permanence was uncertain. Honey did not stick on the walls, attracted ants, and all were removed by water. Tempera, from bird or ostrich eggs, was undoubtedly the most successful, and Johnson found it difficult not to say it must have been the medium used; with it, long thin lines could be painted with all colours. Larger areas of colour could of course have been blocked in by other methods. This experiment was exhaustive, used only local supplies, and was fortunate to find only one possible medium in its search; its conclusions, therefore, are perhaps as near to the truth as prehistoric investigations are likely to get.

A similar type of problem, but one lacking a completely satisfactory solution, concerns the use of varnish in ancient Egypt. The problem was to discover how this was applied to wood. The base of most varnishes is resin, but most of these require a solvent to reduce it to a liquid state; analyses of ancient varnishes show that suitable solvents were probably not available to the Egyptians, and therefore that a resin occurring naturally in a liquid state was probably used. Such a resin is available in pine and larch trees, and are termed oleo-resins; applied warm, they would flow well. In a series of experiments with an oleo-resin of larch (*Larix europaea* or *Larix decidua*), wood was varnished at ordinary temperatures of 20°C and although it took many days to become entirely hard, this seemed to represent the most readily available type of varnish that could be applied (Lucas 1962, 359). However, problems still exist over the actual source of the ancient oleo-resins, and it has been suggested that the characteristic black varnish could only have been procured from certain trees in western Asia which were not available in Egypt. The experiments are a useful reminder that an unknown quantity of ancient materials, sources and supplies are no longer available in their original situations, and are possibly now totally used up or otherwise extinguished.

The ancient Egyptians were probably the first people in the world to make material for writing upon, and the plant used (*Cyperus papyrus*) has provided the word paper. Papyrus is a sedge, growing up to 3 metres high, but under 4 cm in diameter. The stem has a thin outer rind and an inner cellular pith, the latter providing the material for paper-making.

Two successful experiments have indicated some of the ways by which paper could have been made from papyrus in antiquity (Lucas 1962, 137). In an early test, sections of fresh papyrus were stripped of their outer rind, and the pith cut into long slices. These were put in a layer side by side, overlapping slightly, and a second upper layer was identically laid but at right angles to the first; the layers rested on and were covered by an absorbent material. The mass was then beaten with a stone or wood mallet, and then pressed firm; the resultant sheet could be polished with a smooth pebble or wooden tool. Holes could be filled by new slices beaten into place. The second method successfully tested involved the same process, but the strips were more carefully sliced and were laid side by side but not overlapping. The result was essentially the same.

The value of papyrus to ancient Egypt was not restricted to paper. As it was also used for food, fuel, basketry and boats (p. 109), it was one of the few natural materials upon which an early society could depend.

MUSICAL INSTRUMENTS

'Heard melodies are sweet, but those unheard are sweeter . . .'
(Keats)

In the field of ancient music, the words prehistoric archaeology are all too literal; there are no records of the music of prehistoric man by definition, and archaeology is left with the instruments that have survived. These instruments are numerous and represent almost all of the major forms of music-making equipment that are used today, pipes and reeds, strings, horns, and rattles and drums. Some of the pieces are complete, many are in fragments or lack essential parts. Some may be played, some can be restored and played, others are beyond repair.

The tragedy is, however, that although we can produce sounds from these instruments we cannot know if they were those actually heard by ancient man, or the order or intensity in which they were heard, or the occasion on which they were heard. The evidence just does not stretch this far, and although ancient authors have described the general type of noise some instruments produced, their records are without precision or detail, and we are left with the actual instruments themselves, to test and record. And even this is far from complete, as there are many areas of the Old and New World where instruments are known to have existed, but have not survived except in fragments. The famous stringed instruments of Ur, reconstituted from a state of almost total decay, the orchestral pieces of ancient China, in fragments, the variety of Egyptian and central American musical elements, only surviving in representations, all indicate the measure of our loss.

The experimental work that has been done on ancient musical instruments is perhaps the most difficult to conduct without inadvertent distortion of the evidence. Instruments are not mere objects to be manipulated without feeling, insensitive to the occasion upon which they were produced and played. They require as much honesty in testing as any other object whose precise function is unknown, and they cannot be given the benefits of advanced knowledge in virtuoso playing or in modern additions to the instrument. The flute, described as the voice of humanity, does not lend itself easily to dispassionate scientific analysis.

The most spectacular experiment with any ancient musical instrument was that conducted in 1939 in Cairo, when Bandsman James Tappern of the 11th Hussars was summoned and told to blow the trumpet of Tutankhamun for the world to hear (Fig. 36).

Fig. 36
Egyptian trumpeters

His trumpet voluntary aroused the interest and enthusiasm of many thousands of radio listeners of the time, and recordings of his performance have perpetuated the myth of the great range and volume of the silver and the bronze trumpets of the young king of the fourteenth century B.C. However, not to prolong the story, Tappern's performance involved the insertion of his own trumpet mouthpiece into Tutankhamun's trumpets. Without this addition (perhaps completely justified in the circumstances), the trumpets produce only 4 notes between them, and 2 sound very weak and uncertain indeed. The actual notes have been recorded differently on 3 occasions, and tend to wander around c' (middle C on the piano) and d'' for the bronze trumpet and $b\flat$ and c'' for the silver trumpet (Kirby 1946; Megaw 1968, 346).

This event is symptomatic of the dangers in the field of musical archaeology or palaeo-organology as it is sometimes lugubriously called. Any introduction of modern or otherwise uncertain equipment or performance can only invalidate the results, and although

it is enjoyable to produce noises from ancient instruments, only
their own characteristics should be tested.

One of the first experiments with prehistoric musical instruments took place before 1836, when C. J. Thomsen, the founder of
the Three Age system, investigated the 6 Bronze Age *lurer* found
at Brudevaelte in Zealand. Others were tested under the direction
of J. J. Worsaae before 1843, and by the later nineteenth century
tests on not only horns but pipes and whistles were being made.
These experiments concerned the blowing of more or less intact
instruments, and the identification of the notes produced in terms
of the modern equal scale; this of course offers only one guide to
pitch, and fluctuations in pitch may well have been of no concern
to ancient musicians or listeners, just as they are disregarded by
some modern folk singers in various societies. Recent experiments
with musical instruments can do little more than record, with as
much accuracy as is considered necessary, the notes produced by
the employment of techniques of blowing which are considered to
have been within the reach of ancient musicians; this introduces a
main variable at once, to which is added the total lack of information on sequence and occasion.

The earliest known musical instruments in the world are a
group of bone whistles and flutes from late glacial sites in Europe
and dating from about 30000 years ago. The basic shapes are
simple, and flutes of this type occur up to the present day in some
areas, being simple long-bone tubes with holes for fingering (Fig.
37*b*). Such instruments have often been preserved intact, and can
be blown (Megaw 1960). One of the earliest, from Istallosko in
Hungary, has two finger holes on the front and one on the back
of a cave-bear femur, and when blown like a cross-flute it yields
a''', *bb'''*, *b'''* and *e'''*. A much later end-blown fipple flute, from
Malham Tarn in Yorkshire, of the closing centuries B.C., produces
c'''', *c#''''*, *d#''''* and *f''''*, which equals intervals of semitone, tone,
tone; this has led to a suggestion, unlikely in the extreme, that the
Dorian mode thus evident here must represent Greek musical
influence on the Yorkshire moors. All of the flutes tested, and
there are many, indicate conclusively the absence of any early
fixed tonal system.

Panpipes are less well recorded from ancient times, but were in
existence from about 10000 years ago; representations of the pipes
of Pan occur on Iron Age buckets and show from 4 to 7 tubes
making up these fifth-century B.C. instruments. A slightly earlier
and actual example, from Poland, found in a grave with the bones
of an elderly man, perhaps a local *shaman*, consists of 9 pipes

which when reconstituted yielded c''', d''', e''', g''', a''', c'''', d'''', e'''', g''''; this is a two-octave pentatonic scale, and its presence in eighth-century Poland, if musically deliberate, is astonishing (Fig. 37a).

The earliest ocarina, still in the pipe and whistle class, is of the later third millennium B.C., from Austria; this has a single blow hole and characteristic oval resonating chamber, and produces a', $b\flat'$, b', c'' (Megaw 1968). Surviving Maya ocarinas yield 3 notes (Hammond 1972b).

These instruments and others like them are fortunately limited in their potential range of notes, and through experiment we can say with some confidence that the sounds, or some of them, that we hear were heard by ancient man; more than this we cannot say.

Experiments with another class of blown instrument, the reed pipes, are even more restricted, as so little evidence has survived. The recent recording of a Rumanian peasant playing on two barley stalks must surely point to the irretrievable loss of evidence for music that must have existed in the Balkans for perhaps 5 or 6 thousand years. Replicas of the Greek *aulos* have been tested, but important doubts exist about the type of reed used in these experiments, and for archaeology this whole class of instrument is almost beyond recall.

The same can be said for the strings, potentially the group that could tell us more about the organisation of ancient music than any other; the provision of strings indicates a concern with a range of notes, and the maintenance of particular pitch through tuning. By this token, there is no possibility of testing such instruments even had they survived intact; the reconstruction and playing of the Sutton Hoo harp, now said to be a lyre, is visually and musically pleasing but contributes nothing to our knowledge of ancient music so far as can be determined. More satisfaction attaches to the reconstruction of a six-stringed lyre from the 'Grave of the Minstrel' at Cologne, dating from the eighth century A.D., but its notes, its songs and its place in society are all lost. The famous harps and lyres from Ur are similarly decayed, but small harps in Afghanistan today may reflect some of the power and sound of these large Sumerian harps now totally lost to music.

In the percussion section of ancient musical instruments, there are two sources of material. Rattles of clay, probably skeuomorphs of gourds, have survived from Neolithic eastern Europe, some from children's graves (Fig. 37c), and bronze rattles or crotals from the Bronze and Iron Ages of Europe can also be sounded;

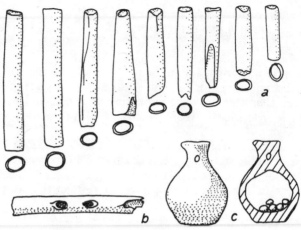

Fig. 37

a Bone pan-pipes, Przeczyce, Poland (1/2)
b Bone flute, Isturitz, France (2/5)
c Pottery rattle, Vychvatincy, Moldavia (1/3)

none contributes much to ancient music. The famous metal bells from Nimrud provide some indication of the clanking and tinkling that went on, and the general racket that must have been heard if all 96 were rung at the same time.

Drums provide important evidence for rhythm in ancient times. Lacking their 'heads' of hide their sounds or sequences cannot be deduced, but replicas of 2 Neolithic clay drums from Bohemia, with calfskin heads (Fig. 38), produced a volume of sound necessitating their recording out-of-doors; the drums are only 20 and 26 cm high (Harrison and Rimmer 1964). The representations of organised clapping in ancient Egypt also speak of rhythmic interests, and combined drumming and clapping sessions have been recorded in recent years along the Nile.

Other percussion instruments include raspers of notched bone, and turtle carapaces struck with the hand or with a beater; one of the latter, a replica of several shown on Maya frescoes, produces 3 different notes by striking the shell in different places (Hammond 1972a), in steel band fashion.

The final group of instruments is the 'brass' section, horns and trumpets of various kinds. There is little doubt that the origin of the horn lies in animal horn-cores with their tips removed; cylindrical tubes of wood are the source of trumpets. The Australian *didjeridoo*, a long hollow tube of wood, can hardly be simpler, but neither can a cow-horn with tip cut off. Experiments on horns and trumpets made of more permanent materials have been numerous, and the results rather more telling than those of other classes of instruments tested and noted above.

The trumpets of Tutankhamun are the best-known of all these instruments but were made with little attention to their mouth-

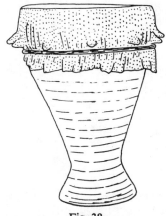

Fig. 38

Replica of late Neolithic pottery drum from Bohemia, with calfskin head (after Harrison and Rimmer 1964)

pieces; the metal of the tubes was merely turned over metal rings, forming a rounded lip comfortable for the performer. Several replicas of these instruments have been made, and the originals have been sounded as well, without additions (Fig. 40g,h). The replicas have also been sounded with extra trumpet mouthpieces to reproduce Tappern's own voluntary, which remains a tribute to the interest in experimental archaeology produced by objects in themselves of inestimable value.

The other instruments that have been tested exclusively are metal horns, made of bronze and brass. It is a tragedy that Greek and Roman instruments have so rarely survived intact, and representations of Roman horns in particular point to the existence of many large and spectacular types. Replicas of the Roman *lituus* and *cornu* have been made and sounded; a *cornu* over 3 metres long produced 17 notes when blown by an experienced musician. One of the few surviving *lituus*, from the Rhine at Dusseldorf, was recently sounded (Fig. 39a); the instrument is only 74cm long, a modest size but with a well-shaped mouthpiece (Klar 1971). The

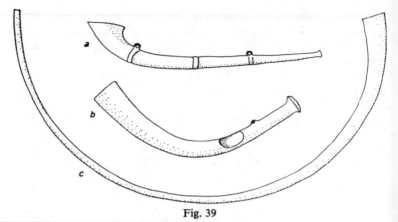

Fig. 39

a Roman *lituus*, Dusseldorf (1/6)
b Bronze Age side-blow horn, Ireland (1/5)
c Celtic horn, Ardbrin, Ireland (1/8)

notes produced, by a professional trumpeter, appear in the table
(Fig. 40a).

An instrument of larger dimensions is the Celtic Iron Age horn
from Ardbrin in Ireland (Fig. 39c); this is 2·4 metres in length,
evenly tapered from the bell for about half its length, then cylindrical to an abrupt end without mouthpiece rounding. The instrument has been sounded with the addition of a plain flat metal mouthpiece, yielding 3 notes $B\flat+$, f, $b\flat+$ (by Radio Eireann, Megaw
1968, 357), but since that date it has been tested without the
mouthpiece, and produces 7 notes (Fig. 40d, Coles unpubl.). The
notes from this horn are almost exactly those yielded by a pair of
Danish *lurer* from Brudevaelte (see below). Another test was made
when the Ardbrin horn was first discovered in a peatbog in 1800;
the horn was in 2 pieces, and when the bell end was blown by the
finder, 'the gong-like noise which it produced attracted the attention of many of the people who resided in the adjacent townlands'
(Petrie 1833).

The largest surviving group of horns is of the Irish Late Bronze
Age, perhaps 900–600 B.C. Almost 100 of these instruments survive, and 25 can be sounded. They are of two types, end-blown
and side-blown; side-blown horns are otherwise unknown except
in relatively modern societies where the solid tip of the animal
horn or ivory has been left on, the hole drilled or cut into the side
of the horn. Most of these have built-up mouthpieces to channel
the player's puff into the horn, but the Irish horns have little or

no aid for this (Fig. 39b); probably a detachable mouthpiece was used, of wood or metal, but none has ever been found. One of the earliest experiments concerning these difficult instruments resulted in the first and only fatality known to experimental archaeology. Dr Robert Ball of Dublin had determined to test these horns, and was able to produce 'a deep bass note, resembling the bellowing of a bull. And it is a melancholy fact, that the loss of this gentleman's life was occasioned by a subsequent experiment of the same kind. In the act of attempting to produce a distinct sound on a large trumpet . . . he burst a blood-vessel, and died a few days after' (MacAdam, 1860).

Of the surviving Irish side-blown horns, 15 can be sounded distinctly (Coles 1963); none can be made to yield more than one note, and the range extends from g to $d'\sharp$, the lowest note obtainable from horns of 80cm length, through a group about 60cm long producing a and $a\sharp$, to horns just over 50cm long with $c\sharp$, d' and $d'\sharp$.

The end-blown horns are either one-piece, or two-piece with a cylindrical tube inserting into a conical bell. Neither has any mouthpiece surviving, but merely a sharp flange over which some sort of shaped tube or mouthpiece was fitted. Of 11 intact horns, a matched pair have cast-on mouthpieces and we can therefore be assured that the sounds produced in testing them are authentically Bronze Age (Coles 1963); the 4 notes obtainable are listed in the table (Fig. 40c). Of the other 9 horns, 7 are short 2-note instruments, yielding fundamentals from $g\sharp$ to $c'\sharp$, dependent upon increasing lengths. Two horns are made up of tubes plus bells, and their lengths are 1·20 and 1·12 metres; one yields 5 notes, and these appear in Fig. 40b. The variable notes that are produced from all the Irish horns, allied to their finished appearance on the outside, and their irregular uncleaned internal surfaces, suggest that it was the presence of the instruments that counted, and that the particular notes produced were not as important. The general clamour that would be heard if all the 24 horns and 48 rattles were sounded on the site at Dowris in central Ireland would no doubt have wakened both living and dead.

The same argument about the lack of musical purity and the emphasis on visual appearance has been advanced for the most splendid of all prehistoric instruments, the north European *lurer* of the Late Bronze Age, 1000–700 B.C. About 50 of these are known to have existed; they are large, from 1 to over 2 metres long, and generally occur as pairs, each pair matched in size but with opposed twists as if to duplicate their original source in pairs of animal

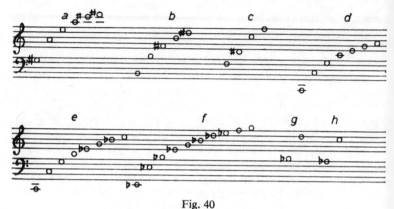

Fig. 40

Notes produced by experiment from ancient horns

- *a* Roman *lituus,* Dusseldorf
- *b* Bronze Age horn, Chute Hall, Ireland
- *c* Bronze Age horn, Drumbest, Ireland
- *d* Celtic horn, Ardbrin, Ireland
- *e, f* Bronze Age *lurer,* Brudevaelte, Denmark
- *g, h* Tutankhamun's trumpets in bronze and silver

horns (Fig. 41). Each horn in a pair of *lurer* is naturally tuned the same as its partner, and therefore the simultaneous playing of a pair would result inevitably in heterophony, or casual accidental harmony. This fact, that harmony was known at this remote time in northern Europe, carried certainly early experimenters rather farther in their assessments than we might care to go today; one statement asserted that the *lur* seemed like a messenger from quite another culture, more developed, finer, as from a people whose taste for the beautiful was at such a pitch that it tried to realise it not only visually, but also audibly.

Various experimental tests on the intact *lurer* have been carried out, ever since the first were found on the Brudevaelte moor in 1797. Recordings have been made of some of the *lurer* on 4 occasions, the latest a comprehensive survey of almost all playable instruments (Nationalmuseet, Danmark, 1966). This was preceded by a full scientific study of their musical potential by G. Skjerne in 1947 (Broholm *et al.* 1949, 81). This showed that 7 to 9 notes could be produced on most of the *lurer*, and were likely to have been within the reach of Bronze Age musicians (Fig. 40*e,f*); professional trumpeters, using all the tricks, could squeeze out up to 16 notes. The mouthpieces on the *lurer* are varied, and in general not very well adapted for the musician's performance. The imperfections inside the instruments also suggest a relative disinterest in the purity of the pitch, and no doubt the simultaneous sounding of the 6 Brudevaelte *lurer* would have produced a most discordant noise, to our ears at least; we do not know of the

Fig. 41

Playing the *lurer* (from *Skalk*, 1961)

musical tastes of Bronze Age people, but all the evidence suggests a ceremonial nature lay behind the production and burial of these enormous instruments. In subjecting them to experiment, however, we should not ignore the enthusiasm with which they have been studied and tested, and in the interest that they, like Tutankhamun's trumpets, arouse in archaeologist and general public alike.

CONCLUSIONS

The value of experiments of the sort that have been described in this book must surely be recognised by all who are concerned with the basic data of prehistory, the surviving traces of man's materialistic past. All manner of his remains can be tested by experiment, by constructing models for examination and assessment, and almost all of the work noted here has contributed something to our understanding of past behaviour, some experiments much more than others, but in no case can proof absolute be claimed. The failure of a piece of equipment to perform an essential task is probably a good measure of its past failure if used in the same way, but the same stamp of certainty cannot be applied to the reverse; the success of a test can only show a possibility, a likelihood perhaps, that an artifact did in fact perform the same function in the past. Yet by such trials and experiments, by such failures and successes, archaeology can profit in great measure in its task of recreating ancient events, in recovering and deducing information about past human behaviour.

Experimental archaeology contributes several elements to any study of the past, an alignment to and familiarity with material culture of all kinds, a range of possible solutions to archaeological problems of interpretation, and an awareness of the many achievements of ancient man. That it lacks the clear ring of truth, of absolute certainty, only aligns it with all other aspects of prehistoric or early historic studies, that archaeologists can do nothing but deal with opinions, with the possibilities and probabilities of past unrecorded events. To this situation, true experimental work can bring an understanding of basic problems that have always taxed mankind, food, shelter, and aids and comforts of all kinds.

Most of the experiments described here have been the work of individuals, from the lone pioneer with his flints or his paints, to groups who collaborate in series testing or with large structures. The field of endeavour is sparse and scattered, and although archaeologists have attempted to gather material together for assessment (Ascher 1961; Proudfoot 1965; Nielsen 1966; Coles 1967), or for bibliographical lists (Graham, Heizer and Hester 1972), there has been little concerted attempt to assemble a body of functioning elements into an experimental centre for continuous testing and for problem-directed work. Recently, several such centres have been established, for example, in Nigeria (Shaw 1966), in Denmark (Hansen n.d.; Nielsen 1966), and England (Research Committee on Ancient Agriculture 1970).

At Little Butser, Hants., an experimental farm has been established on 22 hectares of chalk with green sand fringes. The plan, now under way, is to build several houses and outbuildings, and to run the farm as an Iron Age settlement. There are to be storage pits nearby, and fields are to be ploughed and sown. The success of this experiment will be measured not in one or two years of experiment but over a long term of 10 or 20 years at least, measuring land exhaustion, crops and cropping practices, yields and storage problems, the development of flocks and herds, all in conjunction with a variety of specialist environmental studies.

Of several Danish centres, the Historisk-Arkaeologisk Forsogscenter at Lejre, near Roskilde, now exists as a state-financed project on about 30 hectares of land, including arable, woodland and moorland with water supplies. Structures based on Iron Age and medieval models have been built (Pl. 4), and some of these house light industries producing replicas of ancient objects for study, for display and for sale to an interested public. Small fields for ploughing and planting various crops are laid out beside areas for cattle, sheep and pigs. Much of the raw material for the workshops and experiments is home-produced, wool, flax, wood, meat and grain. The centre serves both as a scientific experimental open laboratory and as a public museum for education and instruction.

The future for experimental archaeology seems to be assured if permanent centres such as these can be established, not only to perform experiments but also to act as repositories for data from other experimental work that will continue on an individualistic basis. The problems of archaeological material are such that the scope for experimental work is almost unlimited, but it would seem, on the basis of work done, that future experiments might well attack some of the basic and developing recovery techniques used by archaeologists on genuine sites, as well as continuing to focus upon food production methods. In other fields, work upon stone transport and the building of monumental structures has been very inadequately tested, although much has been written. Problems of long- and short-distance travel, not only by sea but also by land, are areas of great potential interest for experiment, concerned as they are with population mobility, trade and communication. Reconstructed archaeological sites for observation and excavation would also seem to be a useful aspect for experimental work, and has hardly been touched (e.g. Isaac 1967); its relevance to observations of erosion and decay on recently abandoned camps and steadings (e.g. David 1971) is indisputable. At a lower level, further work on prehistoric pottery manufacture would not be out of place, nor would experiments on the cremation of human or perhaps equivalent bodies. These few suggestions could well be augmented by work on almost any other aspect of material culture and human achievement that has survived, incomplete yet tantalising, for archaeologists to consider in their quest for further insight into past human behaviour.

BIBLIOGRAPHICAL REFERENCES

ABERG, F. A., and BOWEN, H. C. 1960. Ploughing experiments with a reconstructed Donnerupland ard, *Antiquity* 34, 144–7.

ANDERSON, J. R. L. 1967. *Vinland Voyage*. Eyre & Spottiswoode, London.

ASCHER, R. 1961. Experimental Archaeology, *Amer. Ant.* 63, 793–816.

ASCHER, R. 1970. Cues I: design and construction of an experimental archaeological structure, *Amer. Ant.* 35, 215–16.

ATKINSON, R. J. C., PIGGOTT, C. M., and SANDARS, N. K. 1951. *Excavations at Dorchester, Oxon. First Report.*

ATKINSON, R. J. C. 1956. *Stonehenge.* Hamilton, London.

BARROW, T. 1962. An experiment in working nephrite, *J. Polynesian Soc.* 71, 254.

BECHTOL, C. 1963. Sailing characteristics of oceanic canoes, *Polynes. Soc. Mem.* 34, 98–101.

BECKER, C. J. 1962. A Danish hoard containing Neolithic chisels, *Acta Archaeologica* 33, 79–92.

BERSU, G. 1940. Excavations at Little Woodbury, Wiltshire. Part I: the settlement as revealed by excavation, *Proc. Prehist. Soc.* 6, 30–111.

BIBERSON, P., and AGUIRRE, E. 1965. Expériences de taille d'outils préhistoriques dans des os d'éléphant, *Quaternaria* 7, 165–83.

BIMSON, M. 1956. The technique of Greek Black and Terra Sigillata Red, *Ant. J.* 36, 200–4.

BLACKING, J. 1953. Edward Simpson, alias 'Flint Jack', *Antiquity* 27, 207–11.

BLOM, F. 1936. *The Conquest of Yucatan.* Houghton-Mifflin, Boston.

BÖHNE, C. 1968. Über die Kupferverhüttung der Bronzezeit, *Archaeologia Austriaca* 44, 49–60.

BORISKOVSKI, P. 1965. A propos des récents progrès des études paléolithiques en U.R.S.S., *L'Anthropologie* 69, 1–29.

BOWEN, H. C., and WOOD, P. 1968. Experimental storage of corn underground and its implications for Iron Age settlements, *Bull. Univ. London Inst. Arch.* 7, 1–14.

BRAILSFORD, J., and STAPLEY, J. E. 1972. The Ipswich torcs, *Proc. Prehist. Soc.* 38, 219–34.

BRAUNHOLTZ, H. J. 1934. Wooden roulettes for impressing patterns on pottery, *Man* 34, 81.

BRIGHTWELL, A., DEMETRIOU, G., MASSEY, M., and NEACY, N. 1972. The Horniman Museum Kiln experiment at Highgate Wood. Part 1, *The London Archaeologist* 2, 12–17.

BROHOLM, H. C., LARSEN, W. P., and SKJERNE, G. 1949. *The Lures of the Bronze Age*. Gyldendalske Boghandel, Copenhagen.

BROTHWELL, D. 1971. Forensic aspects of the so-called neolithic skeleton Q1 from Maiden Castle, Dorset. *World Archaeology* 3, 233–41.

BROWNE, J. 1940. Projectile points, *Amer. Ant.* 5, 209–13.

BRYANT, G. F. 1970. Two experimental Romano–British kiln firings at Barton-on-Humber, Lincolnshire, *J. Scunthorpe Mus. Soc.* 3(1), 1–16.

BRYANT, G. F. 1971. Experimental Romano–British kiln firings at Barton-on-Humber, Lincolnshire, *Workers' Educ. Ass., Barton-on-Humber, Occ. Pap.* 1.

BURNEZ, C., and CASE, H. 1966. Les camps néolithiques des Matignons à Juillac-le-Coq, *Gallia Préhistoire* 9(1), 131–245.

CALLEN, E. 1967. Analysis of Tehuacan coprolites, in D. J. Byers (Ed.) *The Prehistory of the Tehuacan Valley* 1, 261–89.

CHILDE, V. G., and THORNEYCROFT, W. 1938. The experimental production of the phenomena distinctive of vitrified forts, *Proc. Soc. Ant. Scot.* 72, 44–55.

CLARK, J. G. D. 1963. Neolithic bows from Somerset, England, and the prehistory of archery in north-west Europe, *Proc. Prehist. Soc.* 29, 50–98.

CLEERE, H. 1970. *Iron smelting experiments in a reconstructed Roman furnace*. Iron and Steel Institute, London.

CLOSE-BROOKS, J., and GIBSON, S. 1966. A round hut near Rome, *Proc. Prehist. Soc.* 32, 349–52.

COGHLAN, H. H. 1940. Prehistoric copper and some experiments in smelting, *Trans. Newcomen Soc.* 20, 49–65.

COLES, J. 1962. European Bronze Age shields, *Proc. Prehist. Soc.* 28, 156–90.

COLES, J. 1963. Irish Bronze Age horns and their relations with northern Europe. *Proc. Prehist. Soc.* 29, 326–56.

COLES, J. 1967. Experimental archaeology, *Proc. Soc. Ant. Scot.*, 99, 1–20.

COLES, J. 1972. *Field Archaeology in Britain*. Methuen, London.

COOKE, C. K. 1953. Examination of ash-filled pits in the Magosian deposits at Khami, *Occ. Pap. Nat. Mus. South. Rhod.* 18, 529.

COSNER, A. J. 1951. Arrowshaft straightening with a grooved stone, *Amer. Ant.* 17, 147–8.

COSNER, A. J. 1956. Fire hardening of wood, *Amer. Ant.* 22, 179–80.

COWGILL, U. M. 1962. An agricultural study of the southern Maya Lowlands, *Amer. Ant.* 64, 273–86.

CRABTREE, D. E., and DAVIS, E. L. 1968. Experimental manufacture of wooden implements with tools of flaked stone, *Science* 159, no. 3813, 426–8.

CRUMLIN-PEDERSEN, O. 1969. Kopi af et Vikingeskib, *Skalk* 1969(2), 26.

CURWEN, E. and E. C. 1926. On the use of scapulae as shovels, *Sussex Arch. Coll.* 67, 193–45.

CURWEN, E. C. 1930a. Prehistoric flint sickles, *Antiquity* 4, 179–86.

CURWEN, E. C. 1930b. The silting of ditches in chalk, *Antiquity* 4, 97–100.

DAVID, N. 1971. The Fulani compound and the archaeologist. *World Archaeology* 3, 111–31.

DRIVER, H. E., and MASSEY, W. C. 1957. Comparative studies of North American Indians, *Trans. Amer. Phil. Soc.* **47**(2) 167–456.
DRUCKER, P. 1952. La Venta, Tabasco: a study of Olmec ceramics and art. *Bur. Amer. Eth. Bull.* **153**.
DRUCKER, P., HEIZER, I. F., and SQUIER, R. 1959. Excavations at La Venta, Tabasco, 1955. *Bur. Amer. Eth. Bull.* **170**.
DUNHAM, D. 1956. Building an Egyptian pyramid, *Archaeology* **9**, 159–65.
ENGELBACH, R. 1923. *The Problem of the Obelisks*. Fisher Unwin, London.
ERASMUS, C. 1965. Monument building: some field experiments, *S.W.J. Anth.* **21**, 277–301.
EVANS, O. F. 1957. Probable uses of stone projectile points, *Amer. Ant.* **23**, 83–4.
EVANS, J. 1897. *Ancient Stone Implements, Weapons and Ornaments of Great Britain*. 2nd ed., Longmans, London.
FENTON, A. 1962–3. Early and traditional cultivating implements in Scotland, *Proc. Soc. Ant. Scot.* **96**, 264–317.
FINNEY, B. R. 1967. New perspectives on Polynesian voyaging, *Bernice P. Bishop Mus. Spec. Pub.* **56**, 141–66.
FRANKE, P. R., and WATSON, D. 1936. An experimental cornfield in Mesa Verde National Park, in *Symposium on Prehistoric Agriculture, Univ. New Mexico Bull.* **296**, 35–41.
GARLICK, J. D. 1969. Buried bone, in D. Brothwell and E. Higgs (Eds.) *Science in Archaeology*. Thames & Hudson, London, 503–12.
GLOB, P. V. 1951. *Ard and Plough in Prehistoric Scandinavia*. Aarhus.
GLOB, P. V. 1969. *The Bog People*. Faber, London.
GORDON, D. H. 1953. Fire and Sword: the technique of destruction, *Antiquity* **27**, 149–53.
GRAHAM, J. A., HEIZER, R. F., and HESTER, T. R. 1972. A bibliography of replicative experiments in archaeology, *Arch. Res. Facility, Dept. of Anth., Univ. of Calif.*
GUILLET, E. 1963. *The Pioneer Farmer and Backwoodsman*. Ontario Pub. Co., Toronto.
HAMMOND, N. 1972a. Classic Maya music. Part 1: Maya drums, *Archaeology* **25**, 124–31.
HAMMOND, N. 1972b. Classic Maya music. Part 2: Rattles, shakers, raspers, wind and string instruments, *Archaeology* **25**, 222–8.
HAMPL, F. 1968. Paläethnographie und das Museum für Urgeschichte in Asparn a.d. Zaya, N.O., *Archaeologia Austriaca* **44**, 34–48.
HANSEN, H. O. 1961. Undommelige Oldtidshuse, *Kuml* 1961, 128–45.
HANSEN, H. O. 1962. *I Built a Stone Age House*. Phoenix, London.
HANSEN, H. O. 1966. *Bognaeseksperiment*. Lejre, Denmark.
HANSEN, H. O. 1968. Report of imitative ploughing experiments with copies of a prehistoric ard and with passing-through stilt (Dostrop-type) 1962–8, *Reports from Experiments in Lejre* 1968(1).
HANSEN, H. O. 1969. Experimental ploughing with a Dostrop ard replica, *Tools and Tillage* **1**(2), 67–92.
HANSEN, H. O. n.d. *Historical-archaeological experimental centre—a new Danish research institute*.
HARRISON, F., and RIMMER, J. 1964. *European Musical Instruments*. Studio Vista, London.
HARRISSON, T., and MEDWAY, Lord. 1962. The first classification of prehistoric bone and tooth artifacts, *Sarawak Mus. J.* **10**, 335–62.

HAURY, E. W. 1931. Minute beads from prehistoric pueblos, *Amer. Ant.* **33**, 80–7.

HEIZER, R. F. 1966. Ancient heavy transport, methods and achievements, *Science* **153**, 821–30.

HENSHALL, A. S. 1950. Textiles and weaving appliances in prehistoric Britain, *Proc. Prehist. Soc.* **16**, 130–62.

HESTER, J. A. 1953. Agriculture economy and population densities of the Maya, *Carnegie Inst. Washington, Year Book* **52**, 288–92.

HESTER, T. R. 1972. Lithic Technology: an introductory bibliography. *Arch. Res. Facility, Department of Anth., U. of Calif.*

HEYERDAHL, T. 1950. *The Kon-Tiki Expedition. By raft across the South Seas.* Allen & Unwin, London.

HEYERDAHL, T. 1952. *American Indians in the Pacific.* Allen & Unwin, London.

HEYERDAHL, T. 1958. *Aku-Aku.* Rand McNally, Chicago.

HEYERDAHL, T. 1971. *The Ra Expeditions.* Allen & Unwin, London.

HIGGS, E. S. 1972. *Papers in Economic Prehistory.* C.U.P., Cambridge.

HILL, M. W. 1948. The atlatl or throwing stick: a recent study of atlatls in use with darts of various sizes, *Tennessee Arch.* **4**(4) 37–44.

HOBLEY, B. 1967. An experimental reconstruction of a Roman military turf rampart, *7th Congress of Roman Frontier Studies* (Tel-Aviv), 21–33.

HODGES, H. W. M. 1962. Thin sections of prehistoric pottery: an empirical study, *Bull. Univ. London. Inst. Arch.* **3**, 58–68.

HORVATH, S. M., and FINNEY, B. R. 1969. Paddling experiments and the question of Polynesian voyaging, *Amer. Ant.* **71**, 271–6.

ISAAC, G. 1967. Towards the interpretation of occupation debris: some experiments and observations, *Kroeber Anth. Soc. Papers* **37**, 31–57.

IVERSEN, J. 1956. Forest clearance in the Stone Age, *Sci. Amer.* **194**, 36–41.

JENNINGS, J. D. 1957. Danger Cave. *Soc. for Amer. Arch. Mem.* **14**.

JEWELL, P. A. 1963. *The Experimental Earthwork on Overton Down, Wiltshire, 1960.* Br. Ass. Adv. Sci.

JEWELL, P. A., and DIMBLEBY, G. W. 1968. The experimental earthwork on Overton Down, Wiltshire, England: the first four years, *Proc. Prehist. Soc.* **32**, 313–42.

JOHNSON, T. 1957. An experiment with cave-painting media, *South Afr. Arch. Bull.* **47**, 98–101.

JOHNSTONE, P. 1957. *Buried Treasure.* Phoenix, London.

JOHNSTONE, P. 1972. Bronze Age sea trial, *Antiquity* **46**, 269–74.

KELLAR, J. H. 1955. The atlatl in North America, *Indiana Hist. Soc., Prehist. Res. Series* **3**(3).

KELLER, C. M. 1966. The development of edge damage patterns in stone tools, *Man* n.s. **1**, 501–11.

KIDDER, A. V., JENNINGS, J. D., and SHOOK, E. M. 1946. Excavations at Kaminaljuyu, Guatemala. *Carnegie Inst. Washington, Publ.* **561**.

KLAR, M. 1971. Musikinstrumente der Römerzeit in Bonn, *Bonner Jahrbuch* **171**, 301–33.

KIRBY, P. R. 1946. The trumpets of Tut-ankh-amen and their successors, *J. Roy. Anth. Inst.* **77**, 33–45.

KNUDSON, R., and MUTO, G. R. (Eds.) *Newsletter of Lithic Technology.* Lab. of Anth., Washington State Univ., Pullman, Washington, USA.

LEAKEY, L. S. B. 1934. *Adam's Ancestors.* Methuen, London.

LEAKEY, L. S. B. 1954. Working stone, bone and wood, in C. Singer, E. J.

Holmyard and A. R. Hall (Eds.) *A History of Technology* 1, 128–43. Clarendon Press, Oxford.

LEECHMAN, D. 1950. Aboriginal tree-felling, *Nat. Mus. Canada, Bull.* **118**, 44–9.

LERCHE, G. 1968. Observations on harvesting with sickles in Iran, *Tools and Tillage* **1**(1), 33–49.

LEWIS, D. 1972. *We, The Navigators. The ancient art of land-finding in the Pacific.* Aust. Nat. Univ. Press, Canberra.

LIDDELL, D. M. 1929. New light on an old problem, *Antiquity* **3**, 283–91.

LINNARD, W. 1970. Terms and techniques in shifting cultivation in Russia, *Tools and Tillage* **1**(3), 192–7.

LONG, S. V. 1965. Cire-perdue casting in pre-Columbian Mexico: an experimental approach, *Amer. Ant.* **30**, 189–92.

LOWERY, P. R., SAVAGE, R. D. A., and WILKINS, R. L. 1971. Scriber, graver, scorper, tracer: notes on experiments in bronzeworking technique, *Proc. Prehist. Soc.* **37**(1), 167–82.

LUCAS, A. 1962. *Ancient Egyptian materials and industries.* Arnold, London.

LYNCH, B. D., and LYNCH, T. F. 1968. The beginnings of a scientific approach to prehistoric archaeology in 17th and 18th century Britain, *S. W. J. Anth.* **24**, 33–65.

MARSDEN, E. W. 1971. Greek and Roman Artillery. Oxford.

MAYES, P. 1961. The firing of a pottery kiln of Romano–British type at Boston, Lincs., *Archaeometry* **4**, 4–30.

MAYES, P. 1962. The firing of a second pottery kiln of Romano–British type at Boston, Lincs., *Archaeometry* **5**, 80–107.

MACADAM, R. 1860. Ancient Irish Trumpets, *Ulster J. Arch.* **8**, 99–110.

MCEWEN, J. M. 1946. An experiment with primitive Maori carving tools, *J. Polynesian Soc.* **55**, 111–16.

MACIVER, R. 1921. On the manufacture of Etruscan and other ancient black wares, *Man* **21**, 86–8.

MCLINTOCK, H. F. 1958. *Handbook on the Traditional Old Irish Dress.* Dundalgan Press.

MEGAW, J. V. S. 1960. Penny whistles and prehistory, *Antiquity* **34**, 6–13.

MEGAW, J. V. S. 1968. Problems and non-problems in palaeo-organology: a musical miscellany, in J. Coles and D. Simpson (Eds.) *Studies in Ancient Europe.* Leics. Univ. Press, Leicester, 333–58.

MORITZ, L. A. 1958. *Grain Mills and Flour in Classical Antiquity,* Clarendon Press, Oxford.

MORITZ, L. A., and JONES, C. R. 1950. Experiments in grinding wheat in a Romano–British quern, *Milling* June 1950, 2–4.

MORRIS, E. H., and BURGH, R. F., 1954. Basket Maker II Sites near Durango, Colorado. *Carnegie Inst. Washington, Publ.* **604**.

MUNRO, R. 1897. *Prehistoric Problems.* Blackwood, London.

NANDRIS, J. 1971. Bos primigenius and the bone spoon, *Bull. Inst. Arch.* **10**, 63–82.

NASH, C. H. 1968. Residence mounds: an intermediate Middle Mississippian settlement pattern, *Memphis State Univ. Anth. Research Center, Occ. Paper* **2**.

NELSON, E. W. 1899. The Eskimo about Bering Straits. *Bur. Amer. Ethnol. 18th Ann. Rep.* (1).

NEWCOMER, M. H. 1971. Some quantitative experiments in handaxe manufacture, *World Arch.* **3**, 85–94.

NIELSEN, S. 1966. Eksperiment, *Skalk* 1966(3), 13–23.
NIELSEN, V. 1970. Iron Age plough-marks in Store Vildmose, North Jutland, *Tools and Tillage* 1(3), 151–65.
O'KELLY, M. J. 1954. Excavation and experiments in ancient Irish cooking-places, *J. Roy. Soc. Ant. Irel.* 84, 105–5.
PAYNE, S. 1972. Partial recovery and sample bias: the results of some sieving experiments, in Higgs 1972, 49–64.
PEETS, O. H. 1960. Experiments in the use of atlatl weights, *Amer. Ant.* 26, 108–10.
PETRIE, G. 1833. Ancient Irish trumpets, *Dublin Penny J.* 2, 27–30.
PITT-RIVERS, A. H. 1887. *Excavations in Cranborne Chase*, I.
PITT-RIVERS, A. H. 1898. *Excavations in Cranborne Chase*, IV.
POPE, S. T. 1918. A study of bows and arrows, *Univ. Calif. Publ. Amer. Arch. and Ethnol.* 13(9), 329–414.
PROUDFOOT, V. B. 1965. Bringing archaeology to life, *Advancement of Science* July 1965, 125–33.
PULESTON, D. E. 1971. An experimental approach to the function of Classic Maya chultuns, *Amer. Ant.* 36, 322–34.
QUIMBY, G. I. 1949. A Hopewell tool for decorating pottery, *Amer. Ant.* 14, 344.
RASMUSSEN, H. 1969. Grain harvest and threshing in Calabria, *Tools and Tillage* 1(2), 93–104.
RENFREW, J. 1973. *Palaeoethnobotany*. Methuen, London.
RESEARCH COMMITTEE ON ANCIENT AGRICULTURE 1970. *Prehistoric Farm at Butser Hill: project for research and education*. Br. Ass. Adv. Science and CBA.
REYNOLDS, P. J. 1967. Experiment in Iron Age agriculture. *Trans. Bristol Glos. Arch. Soc.* 86, 60–73.
REYNOLDS, P. J. 1969. Experiment in Iron Age agriculture, Part II, *Trans. Bristol Glos. Arch. Soc.* 88, 29–33.
REYNOLDS, P. J. 1972. Experimental archaeology, *Worcest. Arch. Newsletter* 9.
RICHARDS, A. I. 1939. *Land, Labour and Diet in Northern Rhodesia. An Economic Study of the Bemba Tribe*. O.U.P., London.
RIDGEWAY, W. 1901. *The Early Age of Greece*. C.U.P., Cambridge.
ROBINSON, E. 1942. Shell fishhooks of the California coast, *Occ. Pap. Bernice P. Bishop Mus.* 17(4).
ROBINSON, H. R. 1972. Problems in reconstructing Roman armour. *Bonner Jahrbuch* 172, 24–35.
ROBINSON, K. R. 1961. Two iron-smelting furnaces from the Chibi Native Reserve, Southern Rhodesia, *South Af. Arch. Bull.* 16, 20–2.
ROBINSON, K. R. 1963. A note on storage pits: Rhodesian Iron Age and Modern Africa, *South Af. Arch. Bull.* 18, 62–3.
RYDER, M. L. 1966. Can one cook in a skin? *Antiquity* 40, 225–7.
RYDER, M. L. 1969. Paunch cooking, *Antiquity* 43, 218–20.
RYDER, M. L. 1970. The rural economy of prehistoric Denmark, *Span* 13(2).
SARAYDAR, S., and SHIMADA, I. 1971. A quantitative comparison of efficiency between a stone axe and a steel axe, *Amer. Ant.* 36, 216–17.
SEMENOV, S. A. 1964. *Prehistoric Technology*. Cory, Adams and Mackay, London.
SHAFER, H. J. 1971. Investigations into South Plains prehistory, west central Texas, *Papers Texas Arch. Salv. Project* 20.

SHAW, C. T. 1945. Bead-making with a bow-drill in the Gold Coast, *J. Roy. Anth. Inst.* **75**, 45–50.

SHAW, T. 1966. Experimental archaeology, *West African Arch. Newsletter* **4**, 38–9.

SHAW, T. 1969. Tree-felling by fire, *Antiquity* **43**, 52.

SHAW, T. 1970. Methods of earthwork building, *Proc. Prehist Soc.* **36**, 380–1.

SKJOLSVOLD, A. 1961. The stone statues and quarries of Rano Raraku, in T. Heyerdahl and E. Ferdon (Eds.) *Archaeology of Easter Island.* Allen & Unwin, London, 339–72.

SLATER, E. A., and CHARLES, J. A. 1970. Archaeological classification by metal analysis, *Antiquity* **44**, 207–13.

SMITH, G. V. 1893. The use of flint blades to work pine wood, *Ann. Rep. Smithsonian Inst.* 1891, 601–5.

SMITH, C. S. 1953. Digging up the Plains Indians' past, *Univ. Kansas Alum. Mag.* **52**, 4–5.

SMITH, A. L., and KIDDER, A. V. 1951. *Excavations at Nebaj, Guatemala. Carnegie Inst. Washington, Publ.* **594**.

SOLLAS, W. J. 1915. *Ancient Hunters and their modern representatives.* 2nd ed., Macmillan, London.

SONNENFELD, J. 1963. Interpreting the function of primitive implements, *Amer. Ant.* **28**, 56–65.

SPURRELL, F. C. J. 1892. Notes on early sickles, *Arch. Journ.* **49**, 53–69.

STEENSBERG, A. 1943. *Ancient Harvesting Implements.* Nat. Mus., Copenhagen.

STEENSBERG, A. 1955. Mit Braggender Flamme, *Kuml* 1955, 63–130.

STEGGERDA, M. 1941. *Maya Indians of Yucatan. Carn. Inst. Washington, Publ.* **531**.

STEINBRING, J. 1966. The manufacture and use of bone defleshing tools, *Amer. Ant.* **31**, 575–81.

STELCL, J., and MALINA, J. 1970. *Anwendung der Petrographie in der Archaeologie. Folia Fac. Sci. Nat. Univ. Purkynianae Brunensis. Geologia.* **11**(5).

STONE, E. H. 1924. *The Stones of Stonehenge.* Scott, London.

SWAUGER, J. L., and WALLACE, B. L. 1964. An experiment in skinning with Egyptian Palaeolithic and Neolithic stone implements, *The Pennsylvania Arch.* **34**, 1–7.

THOMPSON, M. W. 1954. Azilian harpoons, *Proc. Prehist. Soc.* **20**, 193–211 (see also Semenov 1954, ix–x).

THOMSEN, E. G., and THOMSEN, H. H. 1970. Precolumbian obsidian earspools: an investigation of possible manufacturing methods, *Univ. of Calif., Contrib. Arch. Res. Facility* **8**, 41–53.

THORVILDSEN, K. 1961. *The Viking Ship of Ladby.* Nat Mus., Copenhagen.

TILLEY, A. F. 1971. An experiment under oars, *Antiquity* **45**, Pl. 10–11.

TYLECOTE, R. F. 1969. Iron-smelting experiments at Varde, Denmark. *Bull. Hist. Metall. Group* **3**, 64–5.

TYLECOTE, R. F., and OWLES, E. 1961. A second-century iron-smelting site at Ashwicken, Norfolk, *Norfolk Arch.* **32**(2), 142–62.

VOCE, E. 1951. Bronze casting in ancient molds. *Pitt-Rivers Mus. Occ. Pap. Tech.* **4**, 112–15.

VOSS, O. 1962. Jernudvinding i Danmark i forhistorisk Tid, *Kuml* 1962, 7–32.

WATSON, P. J. 1969. *The prehistory of Salts Cave, Kentucky. Illinois State Mus. Rep. Invest.* **16**.

WATSON, P. J., and YARNELL, R. A. 1966. Archaeological and palaeo-ethnobotanical investigation in Salts Cave, Mammoth Cave National Park, Kentucky. *Amer. Ant.* **31**, 842–9.

WEINER, J. S. 1955. *The Piltdown Forgery*. Clarendon Press, Oxford.

WHEELER, R. E. M. 1953. An Early Iron Age 'beach head' at Lulworth, Dorset, *Ant. J.* **33**, 1–13.

WHEELER, R. E. M. 1954. *The Stanwick Fortifications. Rep. Res. Comm. Soc. Ant. Lond.* **17**.

WILD, J. P. 1970. *Textile Manufacture in the Northern Roman Provinces.* C.U.P., Cambridge.

WILLIAMS, S. 1968. *The Waring Papers. The Collected Works of Antonio J. Waring, Jr. Papers of the Peabody Mus. Arch. and Eth., Harvard,* **58**.

WULFF, H. E., WULFF, H. S., and KOCH, L. 1968. Egyptian faience. A possible survival in Iran. *Archaeology* **21**, 98–107.

WYNNE, E. J., and TYLECOTE, R. F. 1958. An experimental investigation with primitive iron-smelting techniques, *J. Iron and Steel Inst.* **190**, 339–48.

INDEX